Apple Pro Training Series
iMovie

Dion Scoppettuolo

Apple
Certified

Apple Pro Training Series: iMovie
Dion Scoppettuolo
Copyright © 2015 by Peachpit Press

Peachpit Press
www.peachpit.com

To report errors, please send a note to errata@peachpit.com
Peachpit Press is a division of Pearson Education

Apple Series Editor: Lisa McClain
Project Editor: Nancy Peterson
Development Editor: Stephen Nathans-Kelly
Production Coordinator: Kim Elmore, Happenstance Type-O-Rama
Technical Editor: Klark Perez
Copy Editor and Proofreader: Darren Meiss
Compositor: Maureen Forys, Happenstance Type-O-Rama
Indexer: Valerie Haynes Perry
Cover Illustration: Mimi Heft
Cover Production: Cody Gates, Happenstance Type-O-Rama

ISBN 13: 978-0-133-90095-8
ISBN 10: 0-133-90095-9

9 8 7 6 5 4 3 2 1
Printed and bound in the United States of America

My deepest gratitude to Patty Montesion for all of her help and inspiration.

Climbing to the Tiger's Nest

Contents at a Glance

Table of Contents

iMovie for iOS

Climbing to the Tiger's Nest

34.1s

Getting Started

Welcome to the official Apple training course for iMovie 10 for Mac and iMovie 2 for iOS. You don't need to have any special background to get started, other than having a Mac and/or an iOS device (and perhaps a healthy curiosity about what you can do with home video using Apple products).

Learning iMovie will teach you how to integrate your Mac and iOS device comfortably into your home, school, and work by weaving digital and mobile video into your daily life.

In this book, you'll learn how real people use iMovie. You'll skip some of the more advanced functionality with an eye toward having fun, achieving quick success, and forming a foundation of confidence on which you can build.

What iMovie Does for You

There was a time when your home videos were on a VHS tape in the closet, or just stored somewhere on your computer or mobile device. Organization wasn't even a consideration, so finding a particular video clip was a chore.

But when all your video clips are digital, keeping them organized is streamlined, sharing them is easy, and presenting them in a variety of stunning ways is both simple and fun.

A Mac is designed to function at the heart of your digital life. It's a computer designed for creativity. Your iPhone is one of the most popular cameras in the world. And given that Apple provides iMovie free on all new Mac computers and iOS devices, there is no better time to learn how to take advantage of it all.

What iMovie teaches you is *visual literacy*. The ability to communicate effectively through video is different from speaking or writing. Making high-quality, fun home videos is a skill you can apply throughout your life. Once you develop a few simple editing skills, you'll be stunned by how often you use them, whether for personal pleasure or to your commercial advantage.

Learning software is seldom enjoyable. But sharing video clips or creating home movies, promoting your business, or building a creative video report for school can be fun. You'll end up learning the software along the way.

The Methodology

This book moves through lessons by progressively increasing the complexity of what you do with video clips. You start by viewing and sharing your favorite clips, and then move to creating fun projects like movie trailers. In bonus lessons you'll explore the possibilities of Apple's iCloud with iMovie Theater.

Above all, these lessons are meant to be practical—not esoteric projects to show off the software, but real-life projects for people with time constraints and well-worn equipment. The lessons cover iMovie for Mac and iMovie for iOS in two different sections.

iMovie for Mac

In Lessons 1 through 10, you'll work with video clips from the provided APTS iMovie library. You'll learn how to edit video and share video clips; how to create fun home movies; and how to manage your library of video. In a bonus lesson you learn how to share photos using iCloud with iMovie Theater on the Mac.

iMovie for iOS

In Lessons 11 through 13, you'll get a thorough walkthrough of iMovie for iOS devices. In these lessons, since space is limited on your mobile devices, you'll work with your own video clips as you follow the detailed steps to guide you. You'll learn how to move video clips from your Mac to iOS, how to mark your favorites, and how to share them on popular social networks. Then you'll learn how to create fun, Hollywood-style coming attractions and polished home movies. In a second bonus lesson you'll learn how to use iMovie Theater so that you and your viewers can easily watch your movies on all iOS devices, Mac computers, and even Apple TV.

A Word About the Lesson Content

Often, training materials are professionally created, using actors and complicated productions with multiple cameras and a crew. The resulting material is of high quality but probably bears little similarity to the kind of home video most families have or self-employed business owners can produce.

To make this training as real-world and practical as possible, all the media used in this book was made in precisely the way you would make your own home video. The quality of the video (for better or worse) is comparable to what you can get with consumer video cameras and the iPhone, and the sophistication of the projects is precisely what you can achieve using iMovie, with settings (and challenges) you will commonly encounter yourself.

We tried to make sure the events depicted here were recorded in the way you're being taught to work. Ideally, this will give you clear and realistic expectations about what you can do with your newfound skills.

System Requirements

This book is written for iMovie 10 for OS X Mavericks, which comes free with any new Macintosh computer. It also covers iMovie 2.0 for iOS devices running iOS 7. If you have an older version of iMovie, you'll need to upgrade to the current iMovie version to follow along with every lesson. The upgrade can be purchased through the Mac and iOS App stores.

Before you begin the lessons in this book, you should have a working knowledge of your Mac, its operating system, your iPhone or iPad, and the iOS operating system. You don't need to be an expert, but you do need to know how to use the mouse, standard menus, and the iOS 7 touch screen. You should feel comfortable with opening, saving, and closing files on the Mac, and know how to tap, swipe, and pinch on iOS. You should have a working understanding of how OS X helps organize files on your computer, and you should also be comfortable opening applications on your Mac and iOS device. If you need to review any of these techniques, see the printed or online documentation that came with your device.

Some features require an Apple ID and an Internet connection.

Copying the iMovie Lesson Files

The Apple Pro Training Series: iMovie lesson files must be downloaded to your Mac in order to complete Lessons 1 through 10 in this book. After you save the files to your hard disk, each lesson will instruct you in their use.

To download these files, you must have your book's access code—provided on a card in the back of the printed editions of this book or on the "Where Are the Lesson Files?" page in electronic editions of this book. When you have the code, proceed with the following installation instructions.

For complete download instructions, see "Download Videos for This Book" in Lesson 1.

Resources

Apple Pro Training Series: iMovie is not intended to be a comprehensive reference manual, nor does it replace the documentation that comes with the application. Rather, the book is designed to be used in conjunction with other comprehensive reference guides. These resources include:

▶ Companion Peachpit website: As iMovie is updated, Peachpit may choose to update lessons as necessary. Please check www.peachpit.com/APTSiMovie.

▶ The Apple website: www.apple.com

▶ Apple Pro Training Series books: *Apple Pro Training Series: iPhoto*, by Dion Scoppettuolo, is an excellent companion to this book. Learn how to use iPhoto to enhance your photos, create slideshows, and print keepsake photo books on both OS X and iOS 7. *Apple Pro Training Series: GarageBand*, by Mary Plummer, is an in-depth look at GarageBand, in which you build songs, podcasts, and movie scores from scratch, and explore some of the advanced mixing and arranging features of GarageBand.

Acknowledgements

We would like to thank the following individuals for their contributions of media used throughout the book: Larry Word and the Word family for the Old Home Movies event; Taryn Jaune Glass Blowing for the Glass Blowing video. Leo Bechtold for the Bhutan Tiger's Nest video; Raymond Melcher for the Marlins Spring Training video; and Alexander Blakley for the Max and Louisa in NYC video.

iMovie for Mac

1

Lesson Files	Desktop > APTS iMovie Lesson Files > APTS iMovie Library
Time	This lesson takes approximately 20 minutes to complete.
Goals	Understand the iMovie library
	Download project files for this book
	Navigate the iMovie window
	Switch between your libraries

Setting Up Your Library

Are you the family's hotshot gadget owner with the latest HD camcorder? The screaming-from-the-sidelines soccer mom taking video clips of her kid with an iPhone ? Perhaps you dress in all black, read Jack Kerouac, and make art movies with a digital still camera. Or maybe you just have a lot of cats and sit by the flickering pale blue light of the TV. No matter who you are, you've probably told yourself that you just never have enough time to watch your home videos, much less make a movie from them.

Well, iMovie is about to change all that for you. You'll be making great-looking movies in a very short period of time with fun surprises around every corner. The first 10 lessons go step-by-step through iMovie for OS X and then go on to show you how easy it is to make movies with iMovie for iOS.

Understand the iMovie Library

When you import video clips, iMovie saves them into a library and organizes them into events. Events are like folders containing the clips you import. A library is essentially a larger folder containing all your events. The library is located in your Movies folder, which makes it easy to move all your clips and movies to another Mac or back up to another hard drive.

In most cases, you have only one library, but you can create additional libraries if you choose (for example, if you shoot a lot of video, you may decide to have a library for every year's worth of video).

Let's start by opening iMovie from the Dock.

1   In the Dock, click the iMovie icon.

When you open iMovie for the first time, you'll see the iMovie welcome screen.

2   Click Continue. When the "What's New in iMovie" screen appears, click Get Started.

If you've previously opened iMovie, these windows will not appear, and you may already have an iMovie library with your own video clips in it.

3   Unlike most OS X applications, closing the iMovie window quits the iMovie application, but a more standard way is to choose iMovie > Quit iMovie.

You now have an empty iMovie library for your own personal use, but to follow along with the lessons in this book, you'll need to download the APTS iMovie library and lesson files.

Download Videos for This Book

This book is written as project-based step-by-step instruction. It is designed using a specific iMovie library and media files. You can access the files for this book online.

The iMovie lesson files download includes all the library and media files you'll need to complete the lessons in this book.

To install the iMovie lesson files:

1   Connect to the Internet, navigate to www.peachpit.com/redeem, and enter your access code.

NOTE ▶ If you purchase or redeem a code for the electronic version of this guide directly from Peachpit, the lesson file link will automatically appear on the Lesson & Update Files tab without the need to redeem an additional code.

2   Click Redeem Code, and sign in or create a Peachpit.com account.

3   Locate the downloadable files on your Account Page under the Lesson & Update Files tab.

4   Click the lessons file link and download the **APTS iMovie Lessons.zip** to your Downloads folder.

NOTE ▶ Once you enter the redeem code, you can download the APTS iMovie lessons.zip as many times as you like for your account.

5   After downloading the file, open your Downloads folder, and double click **APTS iMovie Lessons.zip** to unzip it.

6   After unzipping the file, drag the iMovie Lesson Files folder to your Desktop.

The APTS iMovie Lesson Files folder contains the APTS iMovie Library and the lesson files used in this course. Each lesson has its own folder. Note that several lessons use files from a previous lesson; in those cases, the start of the lesson will list the event or existing content used in that lesson.

Navigate the iMovie Window

The iMovie window has four main sections:

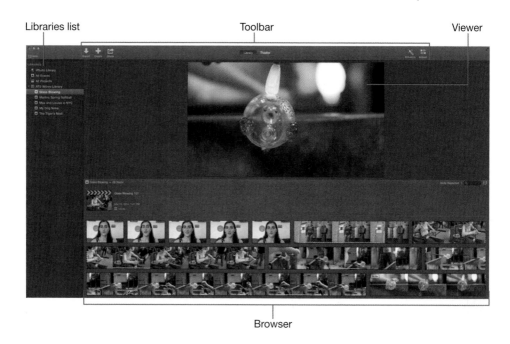

Libraries list   Toolbar   Viewer

Browser

- ▶ The Libraries list shows your clips grouped into libraries and events.
- ▶ The browser displays video clips based on the selection in the Libraries list.
- ▶ The viewer is where you watch selected clips play.
- ▶ The toolbar buttons are used for importing and enhancing clips, as well as creating and sharing projects.

Working with Multiple Libraries

If you've previously imported movies into iMovie, you will already have a personal iMovie library and events in your Movies folder. The APTS iMovie library is located in the APTS iMovie Lesson Files folder on your Desktop. iMovie allows you to work with multiple libraries on the same or different hard drives.

> **NOTE** ▶ For iOS devices there is only one library.

1   In the Dock, click the iMovie icon to open iMovie, if it isn't already.

iMovie opens with your personal iMovie library. You'll need to switch over to the APTS iMovie library.

2   Choose File > Open Library > Other.

3   In the Open Library dialog, click the Locate button.

4   Navigate to your the APTS iMovie Lesson Files folder on your Desktop, and then select APTS iMovie Library and click Open.

iMovie displays the APTS iMovie library in the Libraries list.

You can show and hide the Libraries list at any time.

5   In the toolbar, click the Hide button.

6   To view the Libraries list, click the Show button.

If you're working with more than one library, you may not want to see all the events from all the libraries simultaneously.

7   Click the disclosure arrow next to APTS iMovie Library to hide its events.

8   Click the disclosure arrow again to view the events you'll use in this book.

NOTE ▶ If you want to see only one library in the Libraries list, select the library in the Libraries list and choose File > Close Library > [Library name].

Every time you open iMovie from the Dock or the Applications folder, you will have access to all the libraries iMovie can find on your connected hard drives. When you complete the lessons in the book, you can remove APTS iMovie Library by deleting it from your Desktop.

Lesson Review

1.   Where is the default iMovie library located?

2.   How do I get the library that goes along with this book?

3.   Once I finish the lessons in this book, how do I remove APTS iMovie Library from my Libraries list?

Answers

1. In the Movies folder

2. Navigate to www.peachpit.com/redeem, and enter your access code. Download the files into your Downloads folder. Once the download is complete, double-click **APTS iMovie Lessons.zip**, and drag the APTS iMovie Lesson Files folder to your Desktop.

3. Delete APTS iMovie Library from your Desktop.

2

Lesson Files	Desktop > APTS iMovie Lesson Files > Lesson 02 > Old Home Movies
Time	This lesson takes approximately 100 minutes to complete.
Goals	Get clips into iMovie
	Skim and play clips
	Change the display of filmstrips
	Mark the best and worst clips
	Filter events
	Delete clips from an event
	Play an event full screen
	Share a clip in email

Hide Rejected

Climbing to the Tiger's Nest — 1m 22s

30.0s   34.1s

Lesson **2**

Enjoying and Sharing Clips

Do you want to make movies? Even if you don't, iMovie can still make it fun to watch and share the video clips you record without ever having to make a movie. In this lesson, you'll learn how to sit back and enjoy watching your clips, how to organize clips in events, and how to easily find your favorite clips. Once you've chosen your favorite clips, you'll learn how to share those moments in an email.

Importing Clips into iMovie

Before you can watch your video and share it with friends and family, you need to import video clips into iMovie. Import is the process of copying video clips from a digital video camera, memory card, iOS device, or hard drive into an iMovie library. The library groups clips into events according to the date the clips were recorded.

You'll most often transfer video clips into the iMovie library by connecting your iPhone/iPad, video camera, or memory card directly to your Mac.

> **NOTE ▸** Analog VHS or 8mm camcorders cannot connect directly to your Mac. A detailed list of supported camcorders can be found on the iMovie support website: http://help.apple.com/imovie/cameras.

For this exercise, you'll import clips from a folder. However, you can also use this process for importing from an iOS device or your digital video camera.

1   In the toolbar, click the Import button.

The Import window opens with a sidebar on the left showing all your connected devices and hard drives.

2   In the sidebar, select Desktop.

3   Click the disclosure triangle for the APTS iMovie Lesson Files folder, and then do the same for the Lesson 02 and Old Home Movies folders.

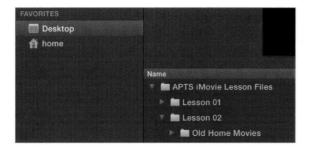

NOTE ▶ iPhoto often opens when you connect a camera or memory card to your Mac. If you don't want iPhoto to open every time you connect a memory card, connect a memory card to your Mac and wait for iPhoto to open, then choose iPhoto > Preferences. In the Preferences window, click General, and from the "Connecting camera opens" pop-up menu, choose "No application." Then close the Preferences window.

All the clips in the Old Home Movies folder are displayed in the lower half of Import window. Before you import them, you want to make sure you know where they'll end up. The "Import to" pop-up allows you to select an existing event to store the clips as well as create a new event.

TIP ▶ Video can take up a lot of space on your hard disk. One hour of HD video (AVCHD or H.264 format) can take up 11 GB of storage. If you plan to keep many hours of video, you should think about investing in a large (and fast) external hard disk.

Events group video clips inside iMovie, much like a folder groups documents. Typically, you'll create a new event for each special occasion you record and name it accordingly.

4   From the "Import to" pop-up menu, choose New Event. (If you have more than one library open, choose APTS iMovie Library as the destination).

TIP ▶ If you have more than one hard drive connected to your Mac, you must create a new library on each hard drive to be able to use it for storing video clips. To create a new library, choose File > Open Library > New.

5   In the New Event dialog, type *California 1950s* and click OK.

The new event is now the selected event in the "Import to" menu.

Now you can select which video clips to copy into your iMovie library. Before you decide which clips to import, you might want to view some first.

6   Click the first clip in the Import window.

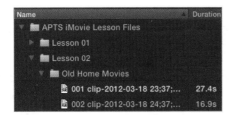

Selecting a clip shows it in the top portion of the Import window.

TIP ▶ When importing from an iOS device or from a digital camera with both still photos and video clips on it, you can choose to show only video, only photos, or both video and photos using the pop-up menu in the upper-right corner of the Import window.

7   Move the mouse pointer over the clip in the top portion of the Import window, then click the Play button or press the Spacebar to play the entire clip.

8   When the clip ends, click the Next button to move to the next clip, and then press the Spacebar to play it.

9   As the second clip plays, click and hold the Next button to fast-forward through the clip.

After viewing a couple of clips, you'll import all the clips from the folder.

10   Select the Old Home Movies folder in the Import window.

11 Click the Import Selected button to import all the clips in the selected folder.

The Import window closes and the process begins, copying the video clips into the library.

12 Click the progress indicator while the clips are being imported to view how much longer it has to complete. (Be quick—this import happens fast.)

The copying happens in the background so you can still view clips in iMovie and check on the progress any time.

The progress indicator disappears when importing is complete. After finishing the import process, the event and all its imported video content are displayed in the browser, ready for you to watch and enjoy.

Skimming and Playing Clips

After you import video clips, they're displayed in the browser as filmstrips. Filmstrips are created using multiple representative frames, called thumbnails. Using the filmstrips, you can quickly see, jump to, preview, and play any portion of any clip.

1 In the browser, move the mouse pointer left and right over the second filmstrip of this mom and the kids in the vintage California scenery.

A vertical orange bar called the skimmer follows the mouse pointer over the filmstrip to indicate your location. As the skimmer moves, the viewer updates to show the corresponding location in the video clip. This process is called *skimming*—a way to quickly find specific parts of your event.

Once you've skimmed to an area you are interested in watching, you can play the clip in the viewer.

2   Position the pointer near the start of the second filmstrip in the event.

3   Press the Spacebar to play the clip.

4   Press the Spacebar again to stop playing.

A filmstrip represents a clip. Clips with a longer duration have more thumbnails in their filmstrip; some longer clips can wrap on the row below.

5   Skim over the first clip until you reach the end of the filmstrip on the right side.

NOTE ▶ Depending on your Mac computer's screen size, the iMovie window and filmstrip display may differ slightly from what is shown in these screen shots.

This clip is extra long. At the end of the filmstrip, a jagged edge indicates that the clip continues on the row below.

6   Move the skimmer down to the row below and continue viewing the vintage scenic California clip starting on the left side of the browser.

Skimming and playing is a good beginning technique, but you use a few other techniques to more easily find the best parts of your clips.

Changing the Display of Filmstrips

If you prefer to change the way the filmstrips appear in the browser, you have a few different ways. One is to change the sort order. By default the browser displays clips by date, with the most recent clips at the top and the oldest clips at the bottom.

1   Choose View > Sort By > Descending.

Now the order is reversed with the oldest clips at the top. The menu has a number of other choices like name and file size as well, but date is probably how you'll most often recognize clips.

If you don't like the look of the filmstrips, you can have a single thumbnail represent the entire clip.

2   Choose View > View > Zoom All Clips.

This menu item collapses the filmstrips into a single thumbnail for each clip. Rather than having only two choices, default filmstrips or a single thumbnail, you can use a Zoom slider to control the length of the filmstrips and the size of the thumbnails.

3   Click the Thumbnail Appearance button.

4   In the Thumbnail Appearance controls, drag the Zoom slider until it shows 2s (2 seconds).

The Zoom slider determines the amount of time represented by each thumbnail in the filmstrip. With the slider set to 2 seconds, each thumbnail represents a duration of 2 seconds. If a clip uses 5 thumbnails (a little math people… anyone?…anyone??)… that's right, the clip would be 10 seconds long. More thumbnails provide greater detail, without having to even skim over the clip. But setting the Zoom slider to show too many thumbnails can cause you to scroll through the browser endlessly.

NOTE ▶ As you work through the lessons in this book, you may want to adjust the Zoom slider and Thumbnail Appearance controls to better match the screenshots in the book.

Let's find a happy medium.

5   Drag the Zoom slider until it shows 5s (5 seconds).

The Clip Size slider determines the size of the images used for the filmstrip. If you're squinting to see the images in the filmstrip, you might need a better camera person— or maybe the thumbnails are just too small.

6   Drag the Clip Size slider all the way to the right.

Now the image size for each filmstrip is extra large.

7   Drag the Clip Size slider about one-third from the left end.

This seems like a decent size where you can recognize what the filmstrip is showing without taking up too much room in the browser.

Marking the Best and Worst Clips

Not all clips are created equal. Some clips are filled with heartwarming, fuzzy goodness, and others are a big waste of time. iMovie provides simple tools to differentiate the two, so you can easily find and enjoy the best parts of your clips.

Selecting a Range and Marking Favorites

With the skimming technique firmly in your grasp, you're one step away from selecting a range within a clip. Selecting a range is the basis for many activities in iMovie. First and foremost, it allows you to identify portions of a clip and to mark them as favorites.

1   On the third clip in the event, skim to the point where the girl in red pants uses the hula hoop.

2   Click and drag to the right on the filmstrip to select about 7 seconds of the clip, indicated by a yellow outline.

The hula hoop is a classic skill practiced by the youth of the time, and it's a very good example, so let's mark this as a favorite clip of ours.

3   Choose Mark > Favorite, or press F.

The green line at the top of the selected range identifies this portion of the clip as a favorite.

If an entire clip is worthy of favorite status, you can mark the entire clip without having to drag out a range.

4   Position the pointer over the fourth clip in the event.

The entire clip of the twin three-year-olds curiously inspecting their first tricycle is a great moment in time. You'll mark the clip as a favorite.

5   Click the clip in the browser. Choose Edit > Select Entire Clip or press X.

The yellow range outline encompasses the entire filmstrip for this clip.

6   Choose Mark > Favorite, or press F.

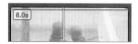

The green line runs along the top of the entire filmstrip for this clip identifying it as a favorite.

If you like to watch your clips instead of skimming through them, you can use keyboard shortcuts to mark ranges while the clip plays.

7   Position the pointer at the start of the sixth clip in the event (dad and son figuring out a birthday toy).

8   Press the Spacebar to begin playing the clip.

9   When the mother first appears on the right side, press I to indicate the start of the range.

10   When the Dad looks up into the camera, press O to indicate the end of the range.

11   Press the Spacebar to stop playing the clip.

Using keyboard shortcuts, you've added a *start point* and an *end point*, marking the start and end of the range, respectively.

12   Press F to mark the selected range as a favorite.

Finally, maybe you're not the type that likes to casually watch your clips and mark them. Maybe being born after 1999 has made you more the impatient, instant-gratification type. For you folks there is a quick way to mark a favorite.

13 Position the pointer at the start of the fifth clip in the event (granddad and grandson playing in the sand).

This clip doesn't feature much action, and it is all pretty much the same. You don't want the entire clip because, well, it gets boring after a while. So you can just mark a section as a favorite part to keep.

14 Begin to skim through the clip and, at any time, press F.

A green line appears from the point of the skimmer forward for 4 seconds. Without marking a range first, you can use this quick and handy way to mark a 4-second section as a favorite.

Refining a Selection Range

Sometimes you'll find that you've selected too much or too little of the clip you want. You can refine your selection before you mark it as a favorite, and you can refine the favorite marking after it has been applied. First let's look at refining your selection range before you mark it as a favorite.

1 Skim the seventh clip in the event (everyone piling on to the outdoor lounge chair).

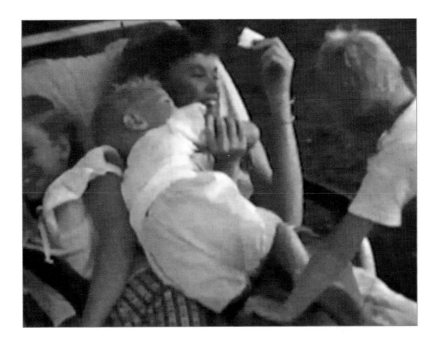

2   Click the clip in the browser. Choose Edit > Select Entire Clip or press X.

The beginning of this clip has a lot of shots with just the tops of heads, and there's even an abrupt jump in the middle of the clip where some of the original film appears to be missing. You'll refine the selection to avoid the first half of this clip.

3   Place the mouse pointer directly over the beginning of the clip, where the yellow outline starts.

The pointer changes to a resize pointer to indicate that you can change where the yellow selection range begins.

4   Drag the start of the yellow range to the right until the duration pop-up shows 10.5s.

The pop-up duration indicates the length of the selected portion. Next you'll look at the end of the selection range.

5   Place the mouse pointer directly over the end of the clip, where the yellow outline ends.

The pointer changes to a resize pointer again.

6   Drag the end of the yellow range to the left until granddad is out of the picture (pop-up duration will be around 8.5s).

7   Press F to mark the selected range as a favorite.

Getting the precise area of your clip marked as your favorite is fairly important. Think of it like highlighting a book. Highlight too much of the book and the highlight is useless; highlight too little and you miss many of the important parts. The same standard applies when marking favorites.

Clearing a Favorite Marking

Another way to make sure you have the exact portion of a clip marked as a favorite is to modify the favorite marking after it's been applied.

1   Skim the eighth clip in the event (the up-close clip of everyone piled on to the outdoor lounge chair).

2   Click the clip in the browser. Choose Edit > Select Entire Clip or press X.

3   Press F to mark the selected range as a favorite.

In a rush to get things marked, you might get overzealous and mark too much of a clip. So the need arises to remove the favorite marking from a portion of the clip. That's why iMovie has a handy "unrate" feature.

4   Deselect any currently selected clips by choosing Edit > Deselect All or pressing Command-Shift-A.

5   Skim to the frame in the clip where the older girl's hand is centered in the viewer.

From here on out, this clip is a blurry mess, yet it is included in our favorites.

6   Drag to create a yellow selection range from the hand to the end of the clip.

7   To unrate the selection, choose Mark > Unrate or press U.

The portion previously marked as a favorite returns to its original unmarked state.

Rejecting Clips

So far you've identified favorite portions of clips, and left some parts unrated. You may also come across portions of a clip you have no interest in. You can hide these undesirable portions in the browser view so you can keep focused on the interesting stuff. The process of hiding portions of a clip uses all the same skills you learned by marking favorites.

1   On the first clip in the event (the girl with the red cowgirl hat), skim over the clip and press X.

This entire clip is just a camera mistake. There is no reason to keep it in the browser.

2   Chose Mark > Reject or press Delete.

The entire clip is removed from the browser, but it hasn't been deleted, just hidden from view.

You aren't limited to rejecting entire clips. As with favorites, you can also reject portions of clips.

3   Scroll to the last clip in the browser (the jumpy scenic clip with the blue and white pickup).

4   Start making a selection when you no longer see the blue truck and the clip starts to get jumpy (about 1.9 seconds in).

5   End the selection at the end of the clip.

People probably have strange sentimental feeling about that old truck so you'll want to leave that but the rest of this clip could cause fits.

6   Chose Mark > Reject or press Delete.

You've successfully rejected an entire clip and a portion of a clip. The rejected ranges are still available if you want them back, but they are now out of the way and no longer cluttering the browser.

Filtering Events

After you've marked some ranges as favorites or rejects, you can filter the event to show only one group or the other.

1   From the pop-up menu to the left of the search field, choose Favorites.

The browser now displays only the portions of clips marked as favorites.

2   From the pop-up menu, choose Rejected.

You can now see all the rejected clips and portions of clips in the browser. The rejected clips have a red line that runs along the top of the filmstrip. If you've rejected an entire clip, you can now go one step further and delete it entirely from your library.

Deleting Clips from an Event

You can save some space on your hard drive by deleting clips you know you'll never watch.

1   While viewing rejected clips, click the cowgirl clip. Choose Edit > Select Entire Clip or press X.

NOTE ▶ You can delete only full clips not portions of clips.

2   Choose File > Move to Trash or press Command-Delete.

3   In the warning dialog, click OK.

The clip is removed from the browser and placed in the Mac OS X Trash. It's still taking up space on your hard drive, so you'll have to empty the Trash to remove it completely and free up the space. To do that you must quit iMovie first.

TIP ▶ If any portion of a clip is used in a movie or trailer, it cannot be deleted. If you press Command-Delete, the clip will disappear from the browser, but it will not end up in the Mac OS X Trash. To get the clip back into the browser, you must first select the clip in the movie or trailer, and then choose File > Reveal in Event.

4   Choose iMovie > Quit iMovie.

The next step is to empty the Finder Trash. Before you proceed, make sure you don't have any personal files in the Trash you don't want to permanently lose.

5   From the Finder menu, choose Empty Trash. Click Empty Trash in the warning dialog that appears.

6   Open iMovie again, and from the pop-up menu, choose Hide Rejected.

You should always review the clips before you move them to the Trash to make sure you really want to get rid of them. Unless you're making backups of all your files, deleting clips accidently can cause you to be ostracized by members of your family.

Enhancing Clips

Now that you have the clips you want to keep and enjoy, it's time to do some quick polishing. Vintage movies like these tend to look faded and washed out. The colors aren't bright, the shadows aren't dark, and sometimes they have an overall blue or orange tint to them. iMovie includes a quick and easy Enhance button to remedy these common problems.

1   Skim over the first clip in the browser (the child riding the tractor tricycle).

2 Click about halfway through the first thumbnail to set the playhead on a clear frame of the child's face (the word *clear* is relative when dealing with 55-year-old home movies).

The playhead appears as a white vertical line that marks the current position in a clip. Unlike the skimmer that always follows your mouse pointer, the playhead is fixed in place unless you click somewhere else in a filmstrip to move it.

When the skimmer is hovering over a filmstrip, it's always used for deciding what the viewer shows and plays. When the skimmer is not hovering over a filmstrip, the play-head is used to decide what the viewer shows and plays. This is helpful in situations like this where you want to see a good representative frame in the viewer but you have to move the mouse pointer to click the Enhance button.

3 Above the viewer, click the Enhance button.

The Enhance button highlights blue to indicate the effect is on. The red of the tractor and the green of the grass have more color now. The shadows are darker and even the child's skin seems less faded. All this with one click—well worth the second it took. In fact, let's apply the Enhance effect to the entire event.

NOTE ▶ The Enhance button also works on audio if an audio track is available and selected.

4   Press Command-A to select all the clips in the browser.

5.   Click the Enhance button to apply the effect to all the selected clips.

6   Press Command-Shift-A to deselect all the clips now that the effect is applied.

7   Skim over some of the clips to see the results.

Although the clips look good, you'll get a much better idea of just how good they look by comparing them without the enhancement.

8   Skim to the clip of the granddad and grandson playing in the sand.

9   Click anywhere on the filmstrip to set the playhead on the clip.

10 Click the Enhance button to turn off the effect temporarily, and then click it again to reapply the effect.

The clip looks like you put it through a washing machine with powerful detergent. The colors look richer, the darks look darker, and the whites look whiter. With all this rich, colorful goodness, you may ask why not always enhance all clips? Well, in some cases it does the wrong thing.

11 Skim to the clip of the sunset.

12 Click anywhere on the filmstrip to set the playhead on the clip.

13 Click the Enhance button to turn off the effect.

This clip looks much better with the effect turned off. The Enhance effect sees this clip as having an overly orange tint to it; in most cases it would be right. On a normal day or inside at a birthday party, this would be too orange. But this clip is a special case. It's a sunset. The Enhance effect does a great job on normal, everyday clips. When the clips are special cases, like this sunset, it's best to avoid the Enhance effect.

Playing Clips Full Screen

With a tidier browser and beautiful-looking clips, you can sit back and really enjoy watching these fun, vintage moments. Although watching them in the viewer is enjoyable, you can play clips full screen for an even better viewing experience.

1 Position the mouse pointer over the viewer to show the play controls.

2   Click the Play Full Screen button to expand the viewer full screen and start playing the current clip.

3   Press the Spacebar to pause playback.

4   Position the pointer at the bottom of the screen to display the play controls.

5   Drag the scrubber left and right to fast forward and rewind through the clip.

6   To go to the next clip in the browser, click the Next button or press the Down Arrow key.

    TIP ▶ Pressing the Previous button or the Up Arrow key will go to the previous clip in the browser.

7   Press Esc to exit full screen.

This lesson so far has been all about finding and viewing the clips you like. The rest of this lesson is all about sharing those clips with others.

Sharing Clips in Email

In general, email isn't the best way to share video because the files have to be smaller than 10 MB (about 30 seconds for a small [non-HD] clip) or your email service will be unhappy with you. But for short little clips like we're viewing in our event, email works just fine.

1   Click the third clip in the browser of the two boys checking out the tricycle.

2   Click the Share button in the toolbar, and then click Email.

In the dialog that opens, you can name the clip, add a description, select a size, and even skim through the clip to make sure it's what you want.

Under the small viewer is an estimate of the file size. The file size is much smaller than the 10 MB limit so you have the option to increase the size.

3   Choose Medium (640 x 480) from the Size pop-up menu.

At its full size, this 8-second clip is still estimated to be only about 512 KB, so you can safely email it without fear of tomatoes being thrown at you from your email provider.

TIP You can add your movie to the iMovie Theater using the "Add to Theater" checkbox. iMovie Theater is covered in a bonus lesson of this book.

4   Click Share.

The file gets formatted for email in the background. After the formatting process is complete, a "Share successful" notification also appears and the movie appears in an email. The clip's name is used as the email's subject.

Although it's tempting to email this clip of someone else's childhood, you probably want to cancel this email and return to iMovie.

You've made you way through the first lesson in using iMovie. You didn't have to make a movie to enjoy and share your video clips. In the next lesson, you'll take the next step and quickly make a movie.

Lesson Review

1. How do you import clips?
2. How do you remove a favorite or rejected marking from a selected range of a clip?
3. How do you view rejected clips?
4. What does a jagged edge on a filmstrip mean?
5. How do you view clips in full screen?
6. How do you know the Enhance effect is turned on for the selected clip?
7. What's the difference between the skimmer and the playhead?
8. True or false? You can delete a portion of a clip by rejecting it and then choosing "Move to Trash."
9. True or false? There is no limit to the size of the movie you can share using email.
10. What do thumbnails represent?

Answers

1. Click the Import button.
2. Select the range and press U or choose Mark > Unrate.
3. From the pop-up menu above the browser, choose Rejected.

4. A jagged edge on a filmstrip means the clip continues on the row below.

5. Click the Play Full Screen button in the playback controls.

6. The Enhance button highlights blue.

7. The skimmer is a vertical orange bar that follows the mouse pointer over the filmstrip. As the skimmer moves, the viewer updates to show the corresponding location in the video clip. The playhead is a white vertical line that is fixed in place unless you click somewhere else in a filmstrip to move it.

8. False. You can delete only entire clips, not portions of a clip.

9   False. You are limited to about 10 MB

10. Each thumbnail represents a duration amount in a clip. The amount each thumbnail represents is set in the Thumbnail Appearance controls.

3

Lesson Files   Desktop > APTS iMovie Lesson Files > APTS iMovie Library > California 1950s

Time   This lesson takes approximately 90 minutes to complete.

Goals   Create a movie with a theme

Add and remove clips in a movie

Place clips where you want them

Rearrange clips in a movie

Audition and add music

Change themes

Share movies to Facebook

Hide Rejected

Climbing to the Tiger's Nest — 1m 22s

30.0s   34.1s

Moviemaking Made Easy

Making a movie sounds like a daunting, expensive, time consuming task. I mean, *Avatar* took 4 years and around $250 million to create! I don't think most of us have $250 million lying around, or have parents willing to chip in even half that. So for the rest of us, we need to find a quicker, less expensive, and easier way to create our masterpieces. In this lesson you'll learn how painless it is to create a great-looking movie in just a few minutes. "Sacre bleu! How can that be?" you may ask, and my answer is by using iMovie themes.

Creating a Movie with a Theme

In iMovie, you create a movie by combining clip selections from an event with titles, transitions, and music. When you apply an iMovie theme, the application places super-swanky titles and transitions in your movie automatically.

1   In the toolbar, click the Create button.

2   From the pop-up menu, choose Movie.

The Create window opens, displaying a number of Apple-designed themes for your movie.

A *theme* is a collection of titles and transitions that conform to a specific style, such as sports, travel, or comic book. You can preview each theme to see if it fits the movie you want to make.

3   Scroll down the list of themes until you see the Playful theme.

4   Hover over the Playful theme and click the Play button that appears on the thumbnail to play a preview.

This theme should work nicely with the vintage clips you're working with.

5   Click the Create button.

6   In the dialog that appears, name the movie *The Golden State.*

7   Leave the California event as the location to save this movie. Click OK.

The iMovie window appears, but the layout is slightly different because the focus is now on making a movie.

There are a few new areas to be aware of in the iMovie window:

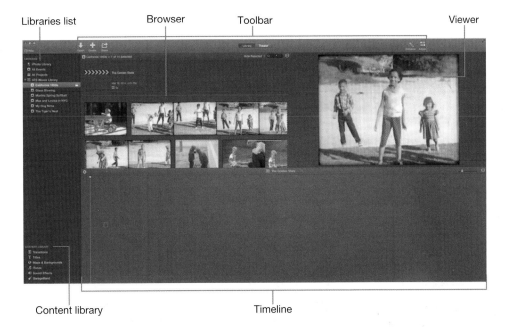

- ► The Libraries list shows your clips grouped into libraries and events.
- ► The content library provides access to titles, transitions and audio you can use in your movies.
- ► The timeline is where you assemble movies and trailers.
- ► The browser displays video clips based on the selection in the Libraries list.
- ► The viewer is where you watch selected clips and projects play.
- ► The toolbar buttons are used for importing and enhancing clips, as well as creating and sharing projects.

Dragging Selections to the Timeline

To create your movie, all you need to do is select the best parts of your videos and drag them to the Timeline window. If you've already marked your favorites, you're good to go. In the current event, some clips are marked as favorites and some you'll choose as you go.

You add clips to a movie by selecting a range and then dragging that selection into the timeline. Since you already marked some favorites in Lesson 2, you'll add those to your movie to start.

1 From the pop-up menu near the browser search field, choose Favorites.

You are now viewing only the few clips marked as favorites. You'll add the favorites to the movie by dragging them to the timeline.

2 Press Command-A or choose Edit > Select All to select all the favorites clips.

3 Drag the selected clips from the browser down into the timeline.

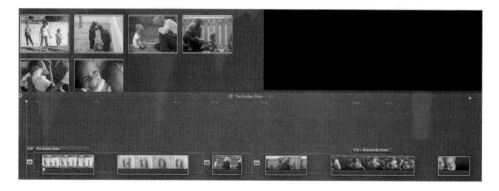

As you hover over the timeline, iMovie shows the outline of the movie complete with transitions and titles. You can release the mouse button anywhere in the empty time-line. If nothing is in the timeline, iMovie always places the first clip at the start of the movie.

The clips are placed into the timeline in the order they appear in the browser. Purple bars above the timeline thumbnails represent the automatic titles produced by the theme. The gray boxes between the thumbnails represent automatic transitions, also produced by the theme.

Let's play the movie to see what it looks like.

4 Choose View > Play from Beginning or press the backslash (\) key.

Nice job! This movie is looking pretty good, although it could use some music (which you'll add later in this lesson).

Dragging clips is the most basic way to add selections to the timeline, but you will learn how to speed up the process in the next section.

Placing Clips Where You Want Them

The start and the end of the movie are a little abrupt. Usually movies start and end with clips that set the scene. To give the movie some context instead of just jumping right into a clip of people, you'll add a scenic clip to the start of this movie.

1   From the pop-up menu near the browser search field, choose Hide Rejected.

Now you're looking at not only your favorite clips but also the clips you haven't marked at all. Some opening and closing scenery clips would help set the scene of the movie.

2   Scroll to the top of the browser.

You'll notice two new things in the browser. First, at the very top is a thumbnail that represents your movie. At some point in the future, when you create additional movies and want to return to view this one, you can always find it at the top of the event you saved it in.

3   Scroll down to the bottom of the browser.

The other thing you may notice under some clips is an orange line, which indicates portions of clips used in the movie.

4   At the bottom of the browser, skim over the last clip showing the California hillside.

5   Skim to about the middle of the clip when the camera starts to pan from the left to the right.

6   Drag the two-headed arrow to the right to create a 4-second selection.

You'll use this 4-second selection at the start of the movie.

7   Position the mouse pointer within the yellow outlined selection.

8   Drag the clip to the start of the timeline, directly under the purple title bar.

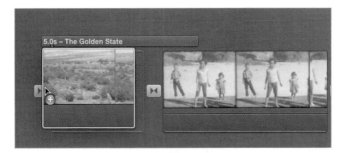

When you drag the clip into the timeline, the timeline thumbnails spread apart leaving gaps where you can drop the new clip.

9   Drop the clip at the start of the timeline, and then choose View > Play from Beginning, or press the backslash (\) key, to play the movie.

   TIP ▶ The iMovie Help menu features a keyboard shortcuts document.

When dragging a clip into the timeline, you don't have to place it at the start. You can drag a new clip between two clips anywhere in the timeline.

10   From the bottom of the browser, scroll up until you find the twins in the toy boat.

11 Skim to the point where the boys are facing away from the camera.

As a general rule of moviemaking, when people aren't facing the camera the scene becomes less interesting, so you'll end the clip with this frame.

12 Drag out a 4-second selection by moving the pointer to the left, so the current frame will be the last frame in the selection.

13 Position the mouse pointer within the yellow outlined selection, and then drag the clip between the first and second clip (hula-hoop girls) in the timeline.

NOTE ▶ When you drag clips into the timeline, you are not copying the actual movie files from your hard disk. The timeline just points to the clips in your event. As a result, you can use a clip in multiple movies without using additional disk space.

The timeline thumbnails spread apart between the clips to create a space where you can drop the new clip.

14 Choose View > Play from Beginning, or press the backslash (\) key, to play the movie.

As you can see, making a movie is incredibly easy. But before you get the popcorn, let's learn a few more tricks to speed things up.

Adding Selections to the End

If you're adding a clip to the end of a timeline, you have a faster way to do it than dragging into the timeline. You can click the Add button to add a selected range to the end of your timeline.

1 In the browser, skim over the clip with the kids in the kiddie bus ride.

2 Just before the clip switches to the boat ride, locate the frame where the child is looking back at the camera.

3 Again dragging backwards from right to left, drag a 3-second selection for the clip.

When you release the mouse button, an Add button appears in the corner of the selection.

You'll use the Add button to append this selection to the end of the timeline.

TIP If the Add button goes away or isn't shown, click anywhere within the yellow selection outline to make it reappear.

4 Click the Add button, or press E, to add the selected range to the end of your timeline.

The clip is added to the end of the timeline, and the ending title bar shifts to move over it. Playing the movie was easy when you wanted to watch the start of the movie, but now that you want to just see the change at the end, you need an alternative to "play from beginning." Similar to clips, the timeline also uses the skimmer and the playhead in the same manner.

5   Skim backwards in the timeline until you see the kids piling on the lounge chair.

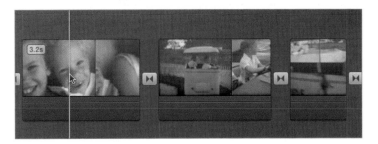

6   Press the spacebar to begin playing from the location of the skimmer.

OK, let's add three more clips to the movie to complete it.

7   In the browser, skim to the sunset clip (after the boys in the boat).

8   Drag out any scenic 4-second selection from this sunset clip, and then press E to add it to the end of the movie.

9   Scroll up in the browser to the twins sitting at a table with the birthday cake.

10 Drag out any 4-second selection you like, and then press E to add it to the end of the movie.

11 Do the same for the next clip after the birthday cake, which shows the water hose fight.

You can see how using the keyboard shortcut can make adding clips a very quick process.

To this point, you've just added clips to a movie. Next, you'll learn the equally important skill of how to remove clips from a movie.

Removing Clips from a Movie

Even after you carefully mark favorites and select portions of clips you want to use in a movie, when it's all put together you'll inevitably notice a clip or two you want to remove.

1   In the timeline, skim over the next-to-last clip of the two boys sitting at the table with the cake.

This clip is pretty dark and not very fun since nothing happens. Let's remove it from the movie.

2   Click the clip of the boys with the cake to select the clip in the timeline.

3   Press Delete.

Deleting a clip from a movie does not delete it from the hard disk, or mark it as rejected. It is just removed from the movie.

Rearranging Clips in a Movie

On many occasions, you'll have the right clips in your timeline, but in the wrong locations. You can rearrange clips to place them in the best storytelling order.

1   In the timeline window, skim over the last clip.

This clip is nice, but the sunset should be the last clip and end the movie.

2   In the timeline, click the sunset clip and drag it to the right, until it's under the purple title bar.

When you drag the sunset clip to the right, the last clip in the timeline shifts over to the left, taking up the former location of the sunset clip. That leaves an opening at the end for you to drop the sunset clip.

3   After you drop the sunset clip at the end of the timeline, skim back to the left until the playhead is over the clip of the boys on the kiddie bus ride.

4   Press the Spacebar to play the movie and review the changes.

Don't be afraid to try different clip arrangements. You can always move clips back to their original positions, or use Edit > Undo to reverse your changes.

Auditioning and Adding Music

Music plays a large part in setting the mood for your video. A head-banging metal song might work with the retro vibe of this movie, but something nostalgic would be more likely to cause a few (sentimental) teary eyes in the crowd.

The content library contains different content you can add to your movie. Audio content is divided up amongst three sources:

▶   iTunes library

▶   Sound effects and royalty-free movie soundtracks

▶   Songs you created in the GarageBand application

> **NOTE** ▶ If you're creating a movie for personal use, you can feel free to use copyrighted music, such as files from your iTunes library. However, if you're planning to share your movie online, it's best to choose from the iMovie royalty-free music library.

1   In the Content Library section of the sidebar, click Sound Effects.

The browser is empty until you select a category to display.

2   Click the filter pop-up menu in the upper left of the browser, and then scroll to the bottom of the menu and choose Theme Music.

The theme music includes royalty-free music clips meant to accompany the various available movie themes.

3   Place the pointer over the Playful theme music, and then click the Play button.

Clicking the play button previews the music and displays it at the top of the browser. The duration for the music is also displayed in a column to the right.

Just above the timeline window alongside the Golden State name, iMovie displays the total length of your movie. This movie should roughly be 50s (50 seconds).

The Playful music is 1 minute long, which makes it a good choice for our 50-second movie. You don't want to select a song shorter than your movie, but if it's a little longer that's OK—iMovie will stop the music when the video ends.

4   Hold down the Command key and click the green music track at the top of the browser.

5   Drag the music track to the background music well, identified by the musical note below the first video clip in your timeline.

6   Release the mouse button when a blue outline appears above the background music well and a vertical yellow snap line appears at the very beginning of the timeline.

iMovie automatically ends the background music track after the last clip finishes or when the music concludes, whichever happens sooner.

NOTE ▸ You can have the music extend beyond the video by choosing Window > Movie Properties. Select the Settings button, and then deselect the "Trim background music" option.

The music track is represented by a green track in the timeline.

7   To play the movie with its soundtrack, choose View > Play from Beginning or press the backslash (\) key.

8   After viewing the movie, to return to viewing the browser, select the California 1950s event from the APTS iMovie Library in the Libraries list.

You can use this method to add as many songs to a timeline as you like. The additional songs will be added to the end of the timeline.

Changing Themes

If you get bored with the theme you've chosen or you just want to try a new one, you can apply a new theme to your movie anytime.

1   Choose Window > Movie Properties.

The Movie Properties show some information about the movie, but to make changes you must open the settings.

2   Click the Settings button.

In these settings you can apply or change a movie's theme.

3   Click the Theme button to open the Create window.

TIP ▶ Choosing No Theme from the Create window will remove the theme from your movie. All titles will be removed as will any theme-styled transitions. Standard crossfades between clips will remain.

4   Click the Photo Album theme, and then click Change.

Yes, I know there are no fireworks or cute sounds to tell you something great has happened, but something great did happen. Your movie has a new look, and in the next exercise you'll experience it in all its full-screen glory.

Playing a Movie Full Screen

When playing a movie you can press the Spacebar to play the movie in the tiny viewer, but when you near completion you might want to see it in full screen.

1   Click the start of the timeline to place the playhead there.

2   Click in the viewer, and then move the pointer to the bottom of the viewer to bring up the play controls.

3   To the right of the Play button, click the Play Full Screen button.

4   Press the Spacebar to stop playback, and then press the Esc key to exit full-screen mode.

You now have a complete movie with a fun nostalgic theme, and the music fits perfectly. Don't horde the beauty of it! In the next exercise, you'll learn one way to share it online.

Sharing Movies to Facebook

A very popular place to share clips is through Facebook. Facebook allows you to post movie files with larger sizes and longer durations than those you can send via email. It also allows your extended Facebook friends and family to view your clips.

1   In the browser, scroll up to locate the movie you just created.

2   Click the movie, and then click the Share button in the toolbar.

3   In the Share pop-up menu, click Facebook.

In the dialog you can name the clip, add a description, select a size, and even skim through the clip to make sure it's what you want.

In the Viewable By pop-up menu, you can set who can view your clip on Facebook.

4   Choose Friends from the pop-up menu so that only you and your friends can view this clip on Facebook.

5   Click the Next button.

If this is your first time sharing to Facebook through iMovie, you'll need to sign in to verify your account.

6 Fill in your account and password information, and then click OK.

The Facebook Terms of Service appear—a fun-filled must-read that covers all the things Facebook can do with your pictures and videos when you post to their site.

If this were your clip, you would click Publish, but it isn't your clip and your friends might think it a bit odd to see someone else's old home movies on your Facebook page. So you can just cancel out of the dialogs to return to iMovie.

Lesson Review

1. What do purple bars in the timeline represent?
2. What does the plus sign on a clip in the browser do?
3. True or false? Deleting a clip from the timeline deletes it from your hard drive.
4. Where, in iMovie, can you find theme music to add to your movie?
5. What does a green track in the timeline represent?
6. If you want to play your project from the beginning, what key do you press?
7. True or false? You cannot switch to another theme once you create your movie by choosing Window > Movie Properties.
8. What button do you click to upload a movie to Facebook?

Answers

1. Purple bars in the timeline represent titles.
2. Clicking the Add button on a clip in the browser adds the clip to the end of the timeline.
3. False. Deleting a clip from the timeline only removes it from the project. It remains in the browser and on your hard drive.
4. Theme music is found by selecting Sound Effects in the content library, then selecting Theme Music from the filter pop-up menu in the upper left of the browser.
5. A green bar in the timeline represents the background music track.
6. The backslash (\) key
7. False. You can change your theme at anytime while you are creating your movie.
8. The Share button

4

Lesson Files   Desktop > APTS iMovie Lesson Files > APTS iMovie Library > My Dog Nima

Time   This lesson takes approximately 75 minutes to complete.

Goals   Choose a new event

Select a trailer

Change the outline

Fill in the storyboard

Remove clips from a trailer

Customize a storyline

Hide Rejected

Climbing to the Tiger's Nest   1m 22s

30.0s   34.1s

Having Fun with iMovie Trailers

Creating iMovie trailers is another simple way to produce an enjoyable, if short, movie. *Trailer* is a term used in Hollywood to describe the coming attractions you see before a feature presentation. iMovie trailers are a slick, fun way for you to turn your clips into bigger-than-life, Hollywood-style coming attractions.

In this lesson, you'll select a movie genre and then customize a storyline to fit your home video. Finally, you'll add clips according to the iMovie storyboard directions.

Selecting a New Event

Before you begin creating a trailer, open a different event in the browser. These clips are somewhat more contemporary than the clips you used in the previous lessons.

1   From the Libraries list, select My Dog Nima. This is an event filled with clips of a small puppy, Nima, taken over the course of a year.

You won't need to see the Golden State movie you created in the previous lesson so you can close the timeline.

2   Click the Close button in the upper-left corner of the timeline, if the timeline is not already closed.

You'll use clips of Nima to make the trailer but first you'll need to change the sort order back to ascending. You may recall that you sorted them in descending order in Lesson 2.

3   Choose View > Sort By > Ascending.

The browser is sorted to show the clips from the earliest to the most recent. You can skim over a few clips to get an idea of what the browser contains.

Selecting a Trailer Genre

Movie trailers are a specific project type that you create in the same way you created the movie in Lesson 3.

1   In the toolbar, click the Create button and choose Trailer from the pop-up menu.

The Create window displays the available trailer templates.

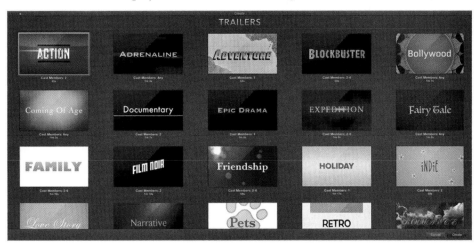

2 Click the Adventure trailer to select it.

Below the thumbnail is information on how many "cast members" this trailer requires and its duration.

3 Click the Play button in the trailer thumbnail to preview it, and then click it again to stop the preview.

> **TIP** ▶ Some of the trailers, such as Blockbuster, Expedition, and Family, allow you to change the number of cast members.

This seems like a good trailer to create for an adventurous puppy.

4 In the Create window, click Create.

5 Name your trailer *Nima and the Dog Bone of Destiny*.

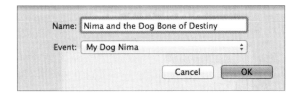

6 Click OK to begin creating the trailer.

NOTE ▶ Unlike with movie themes, you can't switch trailer genres after you begin creating your trailer. To use a new trailer genre with the same video clips, you must create a new trailer.

The tabbed Trailer window appears, and the trailer thumbnail is added to the browser.

Changing the Outline

In the Outline pane, you can personalize the storyline text that accompanies your trailer. You'll be able to customize elements such as the cast list, the release date of your movie, and a studio name and logo. Although every line item in the outline can be changed, the name you typed for the trailer is used for the title. You'll start by changing the name of the lead character.

1   On the Cast Star line, click the name Jake and type *My Dog*.

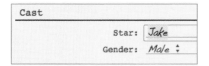

2   Double-click the name Callahan to highlight it, and then type *Nima*.

You'll also need to change the gender so that any titles using pronouns will use the correct pronoun.

3   Choose Female for Nima's gender.

4   Change the studio name to *BOW WOW FILMS* (yes, you're going to carry this dog theme pretty far).

5   To change the studio logo, place the mouse pointer over the Snowy Mountain Peak. The viewing area shows the Snowy Mountain Peak studio logo, which—due to international copyright laws—looks similar but is clearly different from the logo of an actual large Hollywood movie studio.

6   Click the Snowy Mountain Peak text. A menu of alternative imitation studio logos appears.

7   Select Spinning Earth in Space to change the current logo.

8   In the Outline pane, scroll down to view the credits that will appear at the end of your trailer.

9   Move the pointer over the credit text to preview the credits in the viewing area.

By default, iMovie fills in the credit list using the My Card setting in the address book of your Mac, but you can change each credit as necessary. You'll leave that part for later, and move on to adding clips.

Filling in the Storyboard

With the outline personalized, you can move on to the storyboard.

1   Click the Storyboard tab.

The storyboard contains placeholders that describe the types of clips to add, how long those clips should be, and an appropriate clip order. Playing the trailer first without adding any clips is good way to get a sense of what you're creating.

2   At the top of the storyboard, skim to the start of the BOW WOW FILMS title.

3   Press the Spacebar to play the trailer.

The trailer includes titles, music, and all the placeholders you need to create a complete coming attraction. All you need to do is select your best clips to match the placeholder descriptions.

4   Halfway through the trailer, press the Spacebar to stop. Then scroll the storyboard to the top.

The first placeholder is highlighted yellow to give you an indication of the type of clip you need to find. In this case, you want a 2.7-second landscape clip. Clips with a shorter duration will not work. In the browser is a 10.2-second scenic clip, so you'll use that.

5   In the browser, skim over the first clip (the scenery clip) and move your pointer over it.

When the pointer moves over the clip, a yellow selection highlight moves with it. This yellow highlight indicates how much of the clip will be used once you click the mouse.

Adding clips for trailers works a bit differently than adding clips to a movie because the placeholder predefines the length of the clip. So all that is left for you is to decide where the clip will start.

6   Skim along the scenic clip in the browser until somewhere in the middle of the filmstrip.

7 Click the mouse button to add this to the trailer.

The placeholder is filled in with the selected clip, and the yellow highlight moves to the second placeholder in the storyboard.

This next placeholder requires a clip of Nima. This is the first time she'll appear in the trailer, so the clip should clearly introduce her.

8 Skim over the second clip (Nima sitting on gravel). Towards the end of this clip is a nice point where she turns her head from left to right (your left to right, not hers).

9 Skim to the point where Nima starts to turn, and then click to add this clip to the trailer.

This next placeholder in the storyboard is highlighted. This is where the next clip you add will be placed. From the title under the placeholder, it is looking for another a clip of Nima.

10 Skim over the third clip of Nima laying down, yawning.

11 Skim so the yellow outline is located at the end of this clip.

This is a video of Nima yawning—another perfect introductory clip because it's a classic pose of hers (and every dog). It's also a much more close-up clip than the one of her sitting on the gravel.

12 Click to add the third clip to the trailer.

This is a good place to pause and view the trailer so far.

13 Skim to the start of the Bow Wow Films title at the top of the storyboard.

14 Press the Spacebar to play the trailer.

15 After the third clip plays, press the Spacebar to stop playback and get ready to add more clips.

The next placeholder suggests a medium shot. Traditionally in moviemaking a medium shot is usually framed so the bottom of the shot begins at the knees or waist of the subject. How does that translate when the subject is a dog? It's anyone's guess. The beauty of the trailer is that these placeholders are just suggestions. You can follow them loosely and still end up with a fun movie. The fourth clip in the browser is just Nima sniffing around, which will work, but the fifth placeholder is looking for another landscape, which you don't have. So you'll just fill in the placeholders by going in the order they appear in the browser.

NOTE ▶ The placeholder clip description (medium, close-up, long shot) is just a suggestion. You can select any type of clip composition, but the duration cannot be shorter than the placeholder.

16 Click anywhere in the middle of the fourth clip (Nima sniffing around).

17 Click anywhere in the middle of the fifth clip (Nima standing on the red patio).

18 Add the sixth clip (Nima testing the water) by clicking the start of the clip.

19 Use the next two beach clips for the next two medium placeholders by aligning the end of the yellow selection outline with the end of the clips.

20 The ninth placeholder asks for an action clip. Click the next clip at the beginning (Nima running across the floor).

21 Add the remaining clips in the browser by clicking at the start of each one, beginning with the close-up of Nima gnawing on a toy and ending with the shot of Nima being playful on the gravel.

Start with Nima gnawing on the toy.

End with the clip of Nima playful on the gravel.

Your exciting adventure trailer is complete, and you can skim to the beginning and play it to see what you've created. It's a fun movie to watch and really simple to create, but you can still make some changes to improve it.

Replacing Clips in a Trailer

In some cases you may want to replace one clip in the trailer with another one.

1   In the storyboard, skim to the last clip (Nima playful on the gravel).

This clip is very shaky, and you have one more unused clip in the browser.

2   In the upper-right corner of the clip's thumbnail, click the Undo button.

The yellow highlight appears around the now-empty placeholder.

3   In the browser, skim to the last clip of Nima looking across the patio.

4   Skim the clip to locate the point where Nima begins to turn her head, and then click to fill in the empty placeholder.

5   Skim back in the storyboard to the "action" clip of Nima sniffing on the seaweed, and then press the Spacebar to play and see your change.

Knowing that you can change your trailer even after all the placeholders are filled relieves the creative pressure when you're producing your first few cinematic masterpieces.

Using the Clip Trimmer

Although each clip in the trailer has a predefined length, you can change the range used by adjusting it in the clip trimmer.

1   In the Storyboard pane, skim to the "On a Quest for Glory" title. Then skim four clips ahead to the "action" clip of Nima running across the kitchen floor.

This is a nice clip, but her entire running action is missing because the clip ends too soon. Let's try to shift this clip to remove some of the boring beginning frames and add some of the action to the end.

2   Click the Clip Trimmer button.

The clip trimmer opens above the browser and shows a more detailed view of the entire clip, as well as the selected range from the trailer.

3   In the clip trimmer, skim over the clip to view when Nima starts to run. As you can see, the best part wasn't included, so you'll reposition the selected range to include the run.

4   Position the mouse pointer just before the ball leaves the man's hand.

5   Click the filmstrip to the change the selection range, and then click the Close Clip Trimmer button.

6   To view your change, skim back to the "wide" shot of Nima gnawing on the toy and press the Spacebar to begin playing.

> **TIP** ▶ If you want to add more clips than the trailer allows or change a clip's length, you can convert the trailer to a movie by choosing File > Convert Trailer to Movie. After you convert it to a movie, you cannot convert it back to a trailer, so it's wise to duplicate the trailer by choosing Edit > Duplicate Trailer.

The trailer is complete, and you can play it to review what you've created. It's a delightful movie to watch, but you could still improve it.

Enabling Clip Audio

When you add clips to a trailer, the audio from those clips is muted so as not to inter-
fere with the dramatic music. In many cases matching the audio with the storyline of the
trailer is tricky. In our case, adding a bark here or there from the action video clips will
not significantly take away from the drama.

1   In the Storyboard pane, skim to the 1.1-second "wide" shot near the end of the trailer
(Nima on the gravel).

If you skim over this clip, you can see she is barking. It might be nice to add her voice
to her trailer so her fans can hear her.

2   In the upper-left corner of the thumbnail, click the Audio button.

3   To view your change, skim back a few clips and press the Spacebar to begin playing.

The audio adds a little personal touch to this trailer. You can add more of your own personal touch to this trailer by changing some of the storyline Apple provides.

Personalizing the Storyline

You can personalize the trailer's storyline by changing its text. Every line of text in the trailer can be rewritten. In this trailer, the main title at the end reads, "Nima and the Dog Bone of Destiny." That's a dramatic title, but the other titles throughout this trailer are the stock ones provided by Apple. You'll personalize one now.

1   Skim down to the title "On a Quest for Glory."

2   Click the word "Glory."

Most titles are divided into sections based on the style of the text in the title. You can see "Glory" has a different appearance in the viewing area than "On a Quest for." You can change both pieces of text, but Apple divides them up to let you know which text will be in which style.

3   Replace "Glory" by typing *a bone*.

4   Click outside the text box to stop text editing.

> **TIP** After you change text in the storyboard, the right side of the text box displays an Undo button. Click the Undo button to restore the original text.

The changes made in the Storyboard pane can be seen in the viewing area as you type, and you can play the trailer to see the entire movie.

5   Skim to the clip before the title in the storyboard, and press the Spacebar to view your changes.

Trailers offer a unique way to show off your video clips in style. And just like the movie you made in Lesson 3, you can share it to Facebook or another social network supported in iMovie.

Lesson Review

1. Where do you find the choices for movie trailers?

2. How can you change the studio logo at the beginning of the movie trailer?

3. What determines the length of a clip added to the trailer?

4. True or false? Once you add a clip to a trailer you cannot change it.

5. True or false? You can change the trailer style at any time while you are making the trailer.

Answers

1. Movie trailers are located in the Create window when you click the Create button and choose Trailers.

2. Once you create a new trailer, you can select a studio logo from the Outline pane.

3. A clip's length is determined by the placeholder in the trailer.

4. False. You can change a clip in the trailer by clicking the Undo button and clicking another clip in the browser.

5. False. Once you begin creating a trailer, you must start over again if you want to select a new trailer style.

5

Lesson Files
Desktop > APTS iMovie Lesson Files > APTS iMovie Library > Marlins Spring Softball

Desktop > APTS iMovie Lesson Files > Lesson 5 > Leopards Logo.jpg, Marlins Logo.jpg, Damon.jpg

Time
This lesson takes approximately 40 minutes to complete.

Goals
Switch projects in the library

Use the Sports theme

Create sports-oriented video effects

Hide Rejected

Climbing to the Tiger's Nest — 1m 22s

30.0s

34.1s

Creating Your Own Sports Highlights Video

Sports are among the most popular events for families to capture on video. But endless hours of T-ball smackdown don't always make for good popcorn-eatin' video. Why can't our home sports videos look like the highlights we see on TV? Don't we want to add dramatic slow-motion replays and have flying sports graphics? Why not us?

Fortunately, the Sports theme in iMovie is more than a theme—it's a true game tracking, player-highlighting machine!

Switching Projects in the Library

iMovie allows you to make as many movies as you want, and you can access them at any time using All Projects in the Libraries list. You'll begin this exercise with a movie that already has all its clips in place.

1   In the Libraries list, select All Projects.

Every project (trailers and movies) is listed with a thumbnail. When you select a project in the Libraries list, iMovie displays a representative frame in the viewing area. To watch it you must open it.

2   Double-click The First Game movie to open it in the timeline and display it in the viewing area.

Opening the movie from the All Projects category in the Libraries list does not open the event in the browser where all the clips came from. You'll need to do that on your own.

3   In the Libraries list, select the Marlins Spring Softball event.

Now you have the movie and the event showing a kids' softball game. You're going to finish this movie by creating some impressive sports-oriented effects.

Applying a Theme to an Existing Movie

Most of this movie is already completed, but no titles or transitions have been added. You applied a theme when you created a new movie in Lesson 3; here you'll apply a theme to an existing movie.

1   View the existing movie. Press the backslash (\) key to play it from the beginning.

Now you'll add the sports theme to this movie.

2 Choose Window > Movie Properties to display the properties above the viewing area.

3 Click the Settings button to show the editable settings.

4 Click the Theme button to open the Create window.

5 Select the Sports theme, and click Change.

6 Press the backslash (\) key to play the movie from the beginning, and then press the Spacebar to stop viewing after a few seconds.

Not that much happens. By default, when you assign a theme to an existing movie, only transitions and titles you add after you assign the theme are styled based on the theme. Any existing movie elements remain as they were.

TIP ▶ You can change the default behaviors by enabling Automatic Content in the Settings bar. Enabling this option applies theme-styled titles and transitions to your movie.

When you apply the theme without Automatic Content enabled, the Sports theme titles and transitions are not added to the movie, but made available in the content library. You'll add those in a bit, after you create a teams and players list.

Using the Sports Team Editor

You can use the Sports theme as you would any other theme, but if you have a passion for a sports season and record all the games, you can go a few extra yards to make your movie into a real champion. The Sports Team Editor is a database that can track all the teams and players in a season, so when you make your game highlights video, all that information is at your fingertips.

Entering Team and Player Information

You can start entering information into the Sports Team Editor at any time, so don't worry if the season is half over and you have a few movies already started.

1   Choose Window > Sports Team Editor.

The editor is organized into two sections. In the top half, you add and delete teams in the league. The lower half displays the players for a selected team.

You'll start by adding your team to the roster.

2   At the bottom of the Teams section, click the Add (+) button.

A copy of the Leopards team, Leopards 2, is created and ready for you to customize. You can leave the season as it is and change the other information.

3   Double-click "Leopards 2" and type *Marlins*. Press Tab to add Marlins as the second team in the league.

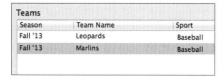

Now you'll change the sport from baseball to softball.

4   Click the word "Baseball" in the Marlins' team entry.

A list of common sports is displayed, but softball isn't there. You'll have to modify the sports list to correct this heinous omission.

5   Click the disclosure triangle next to Sports. A list of sports appears, as well as the stats columns you want displayed for the players in each sport.

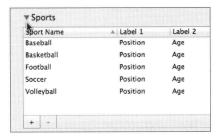

6   At the bottom of the Sports section, click the Add (+) button to create a new sport entry for you to customize.

7   Type *Softball* as the Sport Name, and then press Tab to move to the next column title.

    The columns you create will contain statistics you want to see for each player.

8   Type *Position*, press Tab to move to the next column, and type *Age*.

    You can add whatever stat you want, but using more than 20 letters will cause the text to be very small in your movie.

9   Press Tab again and type *Nickname*.

10   Press Tab to move to the last column and type *Favorite Pro Player*.

    You can now change the sport these teams play.

11   In the Teams section of the editor, set the Sport to Softball for both the Leopards and the Marlins.

    Now that the teams and sport are set up, you can add players.

12   In the Teams section, make sure that Marlins is selected.

13 At the bottom of the "Players for Marlins" section, click the Add (+) button to add a new player entry to the Marlins lineup, ready to be customized.

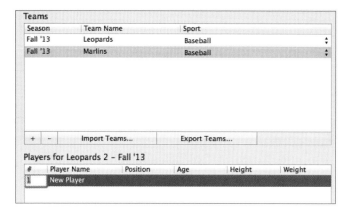

14 Type *26* as the player's number, press Tab, and type *Damon Krupps* as the player's name.

15 Press Tab again to enter his position as *Shortstop*.

16 In the next three columns, set Age to *9*, Nickname to *Prime Time*, and Favorite Pro Player to *Big Papi*.

OK, you've entered the stats for the player, now you can add the team logos and player photos.

Adding Graphics and Player Photos
What would a slick sports highlight show be without personalized graphics of your players and team logos?

1 In the Teams section of the Sports Team Editor, select Leopards.

2   In the Team Logo area, click the Add (+) button.

3   Navigate to Desktop > APTS iMovie Lesson Files > Lesson 05 and open **Leopards Logo.jpg**.

4   Select the Marlins team. In the Team Logo area, click the Add (+) button, and then open Desktop > APTS iMovie Lesson Files > Lesson 05 > **Marlins Logo.jpg**.

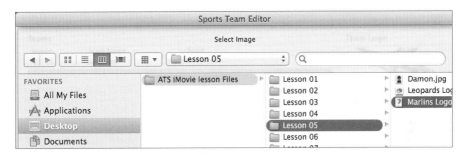

Now you'll add a picture for one of the players.

5   In the Players section of the Sports Team Editor, select Damon Krupps.

6   In the Player Photo area, click the Add (+) button.

7   Navigate to Desktop > APTS iMovie Lesson Files > Lesson 05 and open **Damon.jpg**.

 **TIP** ▶ You can drag photos into the Team Logo well or the Player Photo well instead of using the Add buttons.

You now have the beginnings of a full league database with team logos and player photos and stats. When you assemble your sports movie, you can use all of this information to create championship graphics just like those you see on TV.

Adding Titles and Backgrounds

It's time to put your database to work in a movie. The opening of this movie should show the two competing teams, and with the Sports theme, you have a title that does just that. Unlike in Lesson 3 where iMovie added the theme titles for you, in this lesson you'll add a title on your own using the content library.

1   From the content library, select Titles to display the available title styles in the browser.

The browser shows theme-specific titles at the top and standard titles available to every movie below them.

2   Drag the "Team vs. Team" title on top of the first clip in the movie.

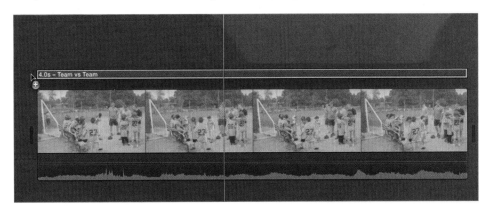

3   Press the backslash (\) key to play the movie and watch the title.

The "Team vs. Team" title is added to the movie and displayed in the viewing area.

NOTE ▶ Because you had only two teams in the Sports Team Editor, those two teams are displayed. To change the participating teams, select them directly in the viewing area from the Team pop-up menu.

You can also choose to add a new team or edit the names of existing teams using the Team pop-up menu in the viewing area.

This title can be placed only over clips. Although this title looks great, it covers up the first clip. You'll fix that by adding a background as the first clip.

4   In the Content Library section of the sidebar, select Maps & Backgrounds.

The browser now shows maps and background selections. Whatever you choose here will not be seen in your movie since the title will cover it up, but you'll choose a simple black background anyway.

NOTE ▶ For more information about adding titles, see Lesson 8.

5   Drag the black background to the left of the first clip in the movie.

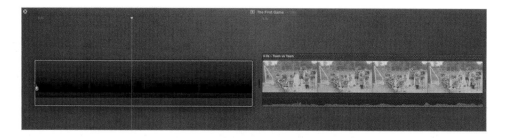

A blue outline makes a place for the background and pushes the other clips in the movie to the right.

6 Click the purple title bar to select it, and then drag it completely over the black background, which is now the first clip in the movie.

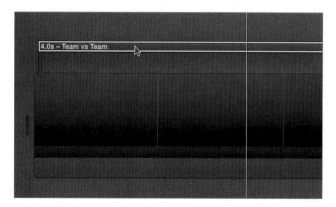

7 Press the backslash (\) key to see the title in action.

Titles are a major part of any sports video, and many of the titles in the Sports theme take advantage of the team and player information you add into the Sports Team Editor. Some titles combine with visual effects to give you the feel of a network sports program.

Creating an Instant Replay Effect

The instant replay should be a key part of any well produced sports highlights show, including yours. An instant replay (for the sports lingo–deprived) is a clip that is repeated at a slower pace to show the action in greater detail and, of course, to increase the drama of a play. Your first step toward creating an instant replay is to find that game-changing event in your movie.

1 Skim over the seventh clip in the movie (counting the black background as one).

This is a good highlight clip of the star player at bat. You can select a portion of the clip to repeat as an instant replay.

2 On the seventh clip, skim to the point just before the ball enters the frame and the player hits the ball (the first time the ball enters the frame he lets it go by).

3   Click and hold the mouse pointer until the yellow outline changes from surrounding the entire clip to just being directly under the mouse pointer.

4   Drag the yellow outline to the end of the clip.

This selection range marks the area that will repeat in slow motion.

5   Choose Modify > Instant Replay > 25%.

The percentage dictates the playback speed. Choosing 25% reduces the normal playback speed by 75%.

In the movie, the clip is extended and the instant replay is added with a title.

6   Skim before the instant replay begins and press the Spacebar to play your new effect. Stop playback once you have seen the entire effect.

That's a classic sports effect every player wants to see himself or herself in. The instant replay and all the speed change options in the Modify menu are available for any movie, but they work particularly well with the sports theme.

Highlighting a Player

You can also single out specific players with graphics that highlight their stats to create a special thrill for them. Once you've entered a player's information in the Sports Team Editor, you can make a Player Stats title to highlight that player.

1   Skim to the start of the clip from which you created the instant replay.

Before the instant replay begins, the clip has a long introduction. This long section before the replay is a good place to show the player's stats.

2   In the Content Library section of the sidebar, select Titles, if the titles aren't already visible in the browser.

3   Drag the Player Stats title on to the instant replay clip, so that the first third of the clip is highlighted in white.

The white highlight indicates the portion of the clip in which the title will appear. You want to display the title in only the first third of this clip while there isn't much action.

When the title is applied, you can select the player you want to highlight.

4   Click the title in the timeline, and then double-click in the viewing area to display the player pop-up menu.

5   Select the Marlins as the Team.

6   Click Done in the upper right of the viewing area to close the pop-up menu.

7   Play the clip to view your title.

Your sports theme movie is complete. Next, you might share your movie with all the players and their families by placing the movie on your iPad, iPhone, or iPod. However, you could also upload your movies to an online sharing site for everyone to access. You'll learn more about posting movies to video sharing sites in Lesson 7.

Lesson Review

1. True or false? Instant replay is available only when using the Sports theme.

2. How do you enter the information for the Player Stats title?

3. How can you access other movies you've created in iMovie?

4. How do you add a team logo to the Sports Team Editor?

5. What sports can be used in the Sports Team Editor?

Answers

1. False. Instant replay fits naturally with the Sports theme but can be used in all movies, with or without a theme.

2. The Player Stats title gets its information from the Sports Team Editor. You must enter all the players and their stats into the Sports Team Editor for the Player Stats title to acquire and display player information.

3. When you want to move from one project to another, select All Projects from the Libraries list.

4. In the Sports Team Editor, under the Team Logo well, click the Add button (+) to import the photo from your Mac.

5. You can add any sports you desire by clicking the Add (+) button at the bottom of the Sports section in the Sports Team Editor.

6

Lesson Files	Desktop > APTS iMovie Lesson Files > APTS iMovie Library > Max and Louisa in NYC
Time	This lesson takes approximately 100 minutes to complete.
Goals	Create a movie
	Replace a clip
	Insert and split clips
	Delete portions of a timeline
	Trim frames
	Connect music tracks
	Work with multiple audio tracks
	Use the clip trimmer with audio
	Set the audio level
	Fade out music

Rejected

ng to the Tiger's Nest — 1m 22s

30.0s   34.1s

Lesson 6
Editing Video and Audio

Feeling a bit more confident? You've created a few very entertaining movies so far but at the risk of popping your bubble, it's time to become a more independent thinker. So far you've let iMovie handle a lot of your decision-making, but if you want to inject more of your own personality into your movies, the next step is to learn about editing clips and fine-tuning audio. Then and only then can you begin to bring your sense of humor and your sensibilities to video clips of the latest hot dog–eating championships.

Creating a Movie Without a Theme

Instead of creating a movie with a theme or filling in the trailer placeholders, in this lesson, you'll create a new movie without all the bells and whistles. You'll postpone the titles and fancy transitions and focus on placing clips into a timeline, removing portions of those clips, and enhancing the remaining content using video and sound effects.

1   Close the First Game timeline if it is still open from the previous lesson.

2   In the Libraries list, select "Max and Louisa in NYC."

3   Click the Create button and choose Movie.

4   In the Create window, select No Theme from the Theme choices.

> **TIP**   You can use the No Theme selection to remove a theme from an existing movie as well.

5   Click Create and type *A Year in New York City* as the name, and click OK.

You'll now select and add multiple clips from the browser to the empty timeline.

6   Click the first clip in the browser, and then press X to select the entire clip.

7   Hold Shift and click the fourth clip from the end of the browser, which shows Louisa with the tutu on her head. Do not select the last three clips.

8   Choose Edit > Add to Movie, or press E.

All the selected clips are added to the timeline in the order they are displayed in the browser.

9   Skim over the timeline and press the backslash (\) key to play the movie from the beginning.

As you play through this short movie, you'll notice that when you add multiple clips at once, you will probably want to make multiple changes.

Editing a Movie

OK, someone needs to say it. Not everyone likes to watch your home movies. It's not that your kids aren't cute, or that your dog isn't incredibly smart, or your vintage movies weren't nostalgic. It's because home movies tend to drag on and on. Here's the good news: It's easy to fix.

Take the time to pick the best clips, and refine and tighten your movie. It makes the difference between a boring movie and something people will truly enjoy watching.

Replacing a Clip

One common refinement is simply replacing clips that may have looked nice in the browser but don't work well in your movie. Instead of deleting the offending clip and separately inserting a new clip, you can perform a single step to achieve both goals.

1   Skim over the first clip in the timeline.

This clip doesn't work as the opening to your movie. It doesn't set the scene or introduce the kids well. The second clip in the timeline is a classic NYC street scene—a clearer way to introduce the city setting. Let's replace the first clip in the movie with another NYC street clip.

2   Towards the bottom of the browser, skim over the rainy New York street clip (third from the end).

This clip is exactly the type you are looking for: a nice, rainy NYC street scene. Because it is only 2.4 seconds long, you'll use the entire clip.

3   Choose Edit > Select Entire Clip, or press X, to select the entire rainy NYC clip in the browser.

4   Drag the clip over the first movie clip. When the white border appears, release the mouse button.

When you drop a clip from the browser directly on top of a movie clip, the Edit pop-up menu appears with a few simple editing choices.

5   From the Edit pop-up menu, choose Replace.

The new clip replaces the old clip in the timeline. The new clip's length is determined by the selection you make in the browser. Replace is a simple yet common edit you'll use often.

TIP ▶ "Replace from Start" and "Replace from End" use the length of the clip in the timeline to determine the duration of the new clip.

Inserting and Splitting a Clip

Insert edits are useful for splitting a single clip into two parts and placing a new clip between those parts.

1   In the timeline, skim over the long clip of Louisa playing in the snow.

This is a very long clip to show uninterrupted. You could use a shorter portion of the clip, but the delightful quality of it is the long, seemingly oblivious back-and-forth traipsing in the snow. You can preserve the fun in this clip and still sustain interest by breaking it up with other clips.

2   In the browser, skim over the snowy park shot, which is the next-to-last clip. This similarly snowy scene is a good clip to insert.

3   Choose Edit > Select Entire Clip, or press X, to select the entire snowy park clip, and then drag it into the timeline window about one-third of the way into the long clip of Louisa.

4   From the Edit pop-up menu, choose Insert.

The snowy path clip splits the longer clip into two sections. You'll insert one more clip to break up the second half of the clip.

5   Skim over the last clip in the browser. This is a seven-second clip of Louisa dragging her snow-filled sled.

6   Choose Edit > Select Entire Clip, or press X, to select the entire clip.

NOTE ▶ Based on the screen size of your Mac and the size of the iMovie window, your filmstrips may appear slightly different from these examples. You can use the timeline's Thumbnail Appearance pop-up menu and Zoom slider to change the size of your timeline filmstrips.

7   Drag the clip into the timeline window, about halfway into the longer, second clip of Louisa in the snow.

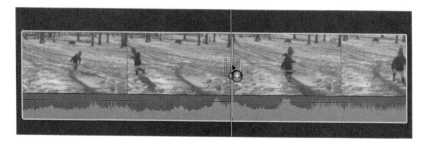

8   Release the mouse button when you're roughly halfway along the filmstrip.

9   From the Edit pop-up menu, choose Insert.

The clip of Louisa and the sled is inserted, splitting the longer clip into two sections. This creates three shorter eight-second clips of Louisa in the snow, split by other snowy clips.

10 Skim back to the start of the first snowy clip and play the timeline to see how the clips flow together.

This winter-in-the-city section is good enough for now. In Lesson 7, you'll give this sequence of clips a little extra distinction using effects.

Deleting Portions of a Timeline

Removing sections of clips that are just too long or unimportant is a fundamental way to refine clips in your movie.

Although there are more precise ways to remove portions of a clip, let's start with the easiest and quickest way.

1   In the timeline, skim to the clip of Louisa chasing a remote control car. It's the fifth clip from the end of the movie.

This clip is a good candidate for editing. All the interesting action happens at the start of the clip, so why not remove the less-interesting ending?

2   Skim to the point where Louisa is no longer onscreen and then back up a tiny bit until you can see Louisa again.

3   Click and hold the mouse button until the yellow selection outline changes from surrounding the entire clip, to just being under the pointer.

4   Drag a selection range to the right from this point to the end of the clip. You should now have about 2.5-second selection range you can remove from the timeline.

5   Press Delete to remove the selected range.

> **TIP** ▶ In this example, you selected the range you wanted to delete. You could also select the range to keep and then choose Modify > Trim Selection to delete the unselected portion of the clip.

The deleted portion is removed from the movie, but it still exists in the browser.

Trimming Frames

Another method of removing portions of a clip in the timeline is the more traditional moviemaking method, called trimming.

1   In the timeline, skim to the clip of Louisa pulling the sled, which you inserted earlier.

This clip has a lot of wasted time before the sled comes into view and after Louisa leaves the view, which makes it a good candidate for editing.

2   Move the mouse pointer to the end of the clip in the timeline.

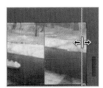

The pointer changes to a trim pointer.

TIP The trim pointer appears when you move the pointer to the start of a clip in the timeline as well as the end of a clip.

3   Drag the mouse pointer in towards the center of the clip until Louisa is back in the viewer.

As you trim the frames from the end of the clip, a help tag shows the number of seconds you are removing from the clip.

Just like when you deleted a portion of the clip in the previous exercise, the trimmed frames are removed from the movie but still exist in the browser. In fact, you can trim away from the center of the clip to return some frames if you feel you have gone too far.

Trimming Frames to the Playhead

The beginning of this clip also needs some trimming. This time you'll use the playhead to set the exact frame where you want the clip to begin.

1   Skim over the beginning of the clip until the sled is fully in the viewer.

This is where you want to begin this clip.

2   Click to position the playhead at this location.

3   Choose Modify > Trim to Playhead.

Since the playhead was positioned in the first half of the clip, frames were removed from the beginning of the clip. If you placed the playhead towards the end of the clip, frames would be removed from the end.

Working with Audio

Always remember that an audience listens to your movie as much as they watch it. Audio's importance is sometimes underestimated, but it remains a significant element in your movie. In this exercise, you'll enhance your movie by adding audio tracks that work well with the video.

iMovie has two types of audio tracks. You've already worked with one, the background music track, of which there is only one. The other tracks are connected audio tracks. Background music tracks are not affected by edits or changes made to other clips in your movie. Connected audio tracks are linked to specific video clips. If you move the linked video clip, the connected audio clips move with them.

Connecting a Music Track

When you added a music track in Lesson 3, it was placed in the background music well, but you can add additional tracks using connected clips. This time you'll add music that starts when Max opens his eyes in bed.

1   In the Content Library section of the sidebar, select Sound Effects.

2   From the pop-up menu above the browser, choose Jingles.

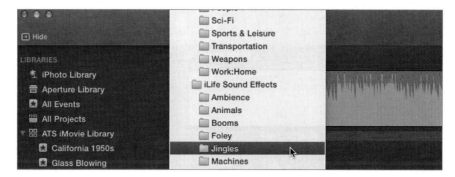

3   Scroll down to find **Piano Ballad.caf**, and then double-click it to hear the song. Click the Pause button to the left of the name to stop.

The light green spiky shape that runs along the green audio track at the top of the browser represents the audio that is playing—the *audio waveform*. The taller the waveform, the louder the audio is during that portion of the audio clip.

> **TIP** ▶ You can access your iTunes music or music from GarageBand by selecting iTunes or GarageBand in the content library.

4   In the timeline, move the pointer to the start of the third clip (Max sleeping in his bed).

5   Click to set the playhead at this location.

The playhead location determines where the music starts in the timeline.

6   Choose Edit > Connect or press Q.

TIP ▶ If the skimmer is present in the timeline, pressing the Q key will connect the clip to the skimmer's location and not the playhead location.

7   Click anywhere in a gray area of the timeline, and then press the backslash (\) key to play the movie from the beginning.

Using the connect edit causes an audio track to connect to the video clip where the playhead is located. In this timeline, since your music track is a connected clip it will always start where the clip of Max starts. If you move the clip of Max to a different location in the timeline, the music will move with it.

Adding Multiple Audio Tracks

iMovie can play multiple audio tracks at a time, which enables you to layer sound effects into your movie. The start of this movie could use some audio to add to the NYC feel.

1   In the Content Library section of the sidebar, make sure Sound Effects is still selected.

2   From the pop-up menu above the browser, choose iLife Sound Effects.

The iLife sound effects include a number of categories for sound effects such as animals, booms, sci-fi effects, and many others. The first clip in your movie is a rainy outdoor NYC street scene, so let's search for some rain storm sounds.

3   Click in the browser search field and type *rain*.

The browser displays all the items in the Sound Effects library containing the word "rain."

4   Click the Play button to the left of Hard Rain to listen to it. This sounds like it would go well at the start of your movie.

5   Drag the Hard Rain sound effect under the first clip in the timeline.

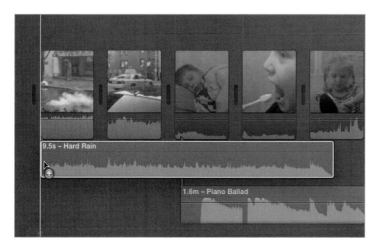

This timeline pushes the music track down to fit the new connected sound effect track.

6   Release the mouse button when the pointer is under the beginning of the first clip in the timeline.

A single green bar is placed in your timeline to indicate the connected audio track that contains the rain sound effect.

7   Press the backslash (\) key to play the rain sound effect. After you've previewed the effect, press the Spacebar to stop playback.

You can add as many connected audio tracks in a timeline as you want. Let's also add some street sounds to enhance the movie.

8   Double-click in the browser search field and type *traffic*.

The browser now shows all the items that contain the word "traffic."

9   Click the Play button to the left of **Traffic.caf** to listen to it. It will work well when played with the rain effect.

10 Drag the traffic sound effect to the same location you placed the rain sound effect.

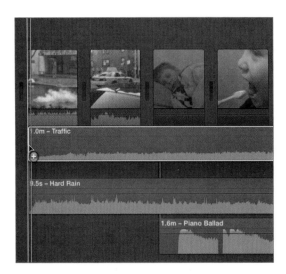

Two green audio tracks now represent the sound effects.

11 Press the backslash (\) key to play the movie, and press the Spacebar to stop playback after you've heard the combination of music and sound effects.

This is a good start at creating the right atmosphere for your movie, but the sound can still be improved.

Trimming Audio Tracks

One of the first things you'll notice about both of the sound effects tracks is that they last longer than the two video clips of the NYC street. In this exercise, you'll trim these two sound effects clips to match the video, and you'll also trim the main sound track to end where the video ends.

1 Move the pointer to the end of the Hard Rain audio track and place it in the top-right corner of the track.

The pointer changes to a trim pointer.

2 Drag the end of the audio track to the left until it is under the end of the clip where Max opens his eyes.

You've now trimmed the rain track to last a bit beyond the opening two street scene clips. You'll do the same to the traffic track.

3 Scroll in the timeline window until you find the end of the Traffic sound effect track.

4 Move the pointer over the end of the Traffic track in the upper-right corner until it changes to a trim pointer.

5 Drag the end of the traffic track to the left until it aligns with the end of the rain track.

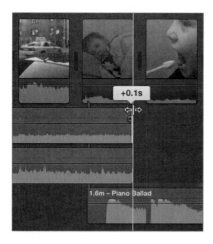

NOTE ▶ The timeline will scroll automatically when you drag over the left or right edge or the window and there is more timeline to show.

6 Play the movie to hear the results, and then stop playback.

You now have consistent rain and street sounds that unite the two opening clips in the movie.

Muting Audio

Some sequences will have a stronger impact if you reduce or entirely remove the clips' original audio. Lowering the sound until it can no longer be heard is called *muting*.

1   Select the first video clip in the timeline.

2   Shift-click the second clip in the timeline to highlight both clips.

With the new sound effects in place, you no longer need the sound from the video clips.

3   In the toolbar, click the Adjustment button, and then click the Volume button.

4   Click the Mute button.

> **TIP**   Clicking the Mute button again when you select muted clips will unmute the clips.

5   Play the timeline to hear the difference, and then stop playback.

Now the sound is embellished and clear because all you hear are the sound effects you added to the sequence.

Using the Clip Trimmer for Audio

During the opening, cars go by but the traffic sound effect just doesn't match up with those passing vehicles. Just because the sound effect is placed at the start of the timeline, it doesn't mean that you have to use the first part of the sound effect clip. You can use the clip trimmer to select a different portion of the sound effect to play in the movie.

1   Select the Traffic sound effect track in the timeline then choose Window > Show Clip trimmer to open the Clip trimmer above the timeline. (You may need to scroll the timeline window up to see the clip trimmer.)

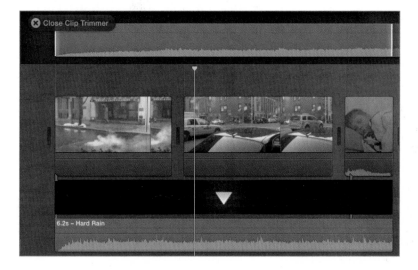

The clip trimmer allows you to see how much of the audio clip is used in the timeline and maybe more importantly, how much is unused. The area between the two white vertical lines is the current selection playing in the timeline. The darker area outside the white selection lines is the remaining portion of the audio clip.

Dragging the audio track within the range in the clip trimmer will allow you to keep the sound effect the same length in the timeline but change the portion of the sound effect clip you're using.

2   Place the pointer in the center of the clip trimmer filmstrip and drag the track to the left until the taller section (the louder section) of the audio waveform is centered within the highlighted area.

TIP ▶ You can enable audio skimming from the View menu to hear the traffic noise as you skim over the clip trimmer.

3   Click Close Clip Trimmer.

4   Play the movie to hear the results, and stop playback when you're done.

Small, detail-oriented adjustments like these can really make a movie feel polished.

Setting a Clip's Audio Level

Not every clip's audio needs to be muted or replaced. Some background sounds, such as the key turning in the lock and the leaves being kicked, add to the ambience of the movie. Still, these aren't the type of sound effects you play at full blast. You can adjust the level of any clip using the timeline volume control.

1   Play from the start of the timeline and stop playback when you hear the sound of the leaves being kicked.

This is a good, natural sound that suits the video, but it is very loud and drowns out the soothing music.

2   On the kicking leaves clip, drag the audio volume control line down to around 20%.

> **TIP** ▶ You can also access the volume control by clicking the Adjustment button in the toolbar, and then clicking the Volume button.

3   Skim to the clip before the kicked leaves and press the Spacebar to start playback.

4   Press the Spacebar again to stop playing after you hear the new audio level.

You may find other locations in the timeline where a clip's audio level could be lowered, still other places where you could mute the audio. Go through your movie and practice adjusting clip levels and muting clips where you think it is appropriate. Remember you can select multiple clips and set their audio level all at once.

Fading Out Music

The music is a bit long for this video. Trimming by itself will just cause an abrupt ending—not what you want for such a mellow movie. If you trim the music closer to the video ending, you can smooth the ending by fading it out.

1   Skim to the end of the timeline.

2   Position the pointer at the end of the music track as if you are going to trim it.

3   Place the pointer over the volume control, where the pointer changes to a fade pointer and the circular fade handle highlights.

4   Drag the fade handle in towards the center of the clip until it is under the start of the last video clip, Louisa with the tutu on her head (a little over 17 seconds).

> **TIP** ▶ You can drag the fade handle at the start of an audio clip to fade in.

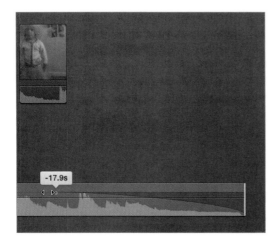

5   Skim backward to the next-to-last video clip in the timeline and press the Spacebar to hear the music fade out.

That's pretty good, but it will sound even better if you trim the music closer to the end of the video. You'll trim it just after the video and let it fade out while the video is black.

6   Move the pointer to the end of the music audio track.

7   With the trip pointer, drag the music track in towards the center of the clip until the pop-up displays about –13 seconds.

8   Skim backward to the next-to-last video clip in the timeline and press the Spacebar to hear the music fade out.

That's a much more timely ending to our mellow NYC movie. In the next lesson, you'll continue with this movie and learn how to enhance the look of these video clips.

Lesson Review

1.   Where can you choose replace and insert edits?
2.   How do you create a movie without a theme?
3.   True or false? When you delete a clip from the timeline, it becomes rejected.
4.   How do you access the trim pointer to trim the end of a clip?
5.   How does a connected audio track differ from the background music track?
6.   True or false? You can have only one background music track and one connected audio track.
7.   How do you mute an audio track?

Answers

1.   When you drop one clip from your event directly on top of a timeline clip, the pop-up menu appears with Replace and Insert edit choices.
2.   Choose No Theme from the Create window.
3.   False. Deleting a clip from the timeline removes it from the timeline only. It still remains in the browser.
4.   Move the pointer over the end of a clip.
5.   Connected audio tracks are connected to a video clip. If you move the video clip to a different location in the timeline, the audio track will move with it.
6.   False. You can have only one background music track, but you can have many connected audio tracks.
7.   Select the audio track you want to mute. Click the Adjustment button in the toolbar, click the Volume button, and then click the Mute button.

7

Lesson Files   Desktop > APTS iMovie Lesson Files > APTS iMovie Library >
Max and Louisa in NYC

Time   This lesson takes approximately 100 minutes to complete.

Goals   Use video effects

Preview and modify transitions

Change the speed of a clip

Enhance video

Fix color problems

Stabilize a clip

Work with titles

Share movies online

ng to the Tiger's Nest — 1m 22s

Rejected

Fixing and Refining the Look

Until now you've focused on adding, removing, replacing, and trimming clips within a movie. Those tasks are considered the fundamental techniques of moviemaking. However, you can elevate your movies when you enhance and fix the look of the clips.

In this lesson you'll continue working on the movie you created in Lesson 6. You'll enhance the story you're telling using effects and transitions. Then you'll fix a few common problems that come up in many home videos.

Using Video Effects

Video effects can change the look of clips to mimic the appearance of Hollywood movies. You can apply simple color effects, such as Sepia or Black & White, or you can use more sophisticated effects such as Dream and Bleach Bypass. You can apply only one video effect at a time in iMovie, but it's easy to try them out.

Your movie started out with New York City and the kids slowly waking up. Then, with a burst of energy, the action moved outside. To embellish the contrast, you'll apply a video effect to the first part of the movie. You'll start by applying an effect to one clip.

1   Select the "Max and Louisa in NYC" event from the previous lesson, and then double-click the project you created to open it in the timeline.

   NOTE ▸ In order to start this lesson, you must have completed editing the movie from the previous lesson.

2   Click to select the first clip in the timeline.

3   In the toolbar above the viewing area, click the Adjust button.

4   Click the Video and audio effects button, and then click the Video Effect button, which currently says None.

All the video effects appear displayed as thumbnails. To preview one, you can move the mouse pointer over a thumbnail and watch it play in the viewing area.

5   Position the mouse pointer over Aged Film, Dream, and Romantic to view each effect in the viewing area.

NOTE ▶ You can stop playback and skim over the effect thumbnail to preview it faster or slower.

6   Press the Spacebar to stop playback and skim over the Black & White effect.

7   Click Black & White to apply the effect to the clip.

TIP ▶ As with transitions, use video effects to enhance the story; don't let them become the center of the story.

Although you can apply only one effect to a clip, you can change the applied effect at any time.

Copying and Pasting Effects

Now you'd like to have the Black & White effect applied to the next six clips that make up the opening of your movie. iMovie provides a fast way to apply a video effect from one clip to many clips using copy and paste.

1   Select the first clip in the timeline, if necessary.

2 Choose Edit > Copy.

3 Click the second clip in the timeline to select it.

4 Shift-click the clip of the key turning in the door lock.

NOTE ▶ Holding down the Shift key selects all the clips between the two clips you click.

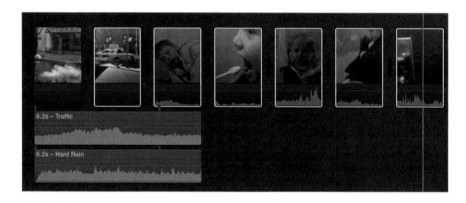

5 Choose Edit > Paste Adjustments > Video Effect. In the Paste Adjustments submenu, you see the options you can paste to the selected clips.

iMovie copies the Black & White effect from the first clip and pastes it to all the selected clips.

6   Click the Play button, or press the backslash (\) key to play the movie.

7   Press the Spacebar to stop playback when the black-and-white section ends.

Pasting adjustments can obviously save a lot of time. Next time you use it, take a moment to view the other pasting options available.

Previewing and Modifying Transitions

When you're ready to add transitions, you can preview them in the same way you previewed video effects.

1   In the Content Library section of the sidebar, select Transitions.

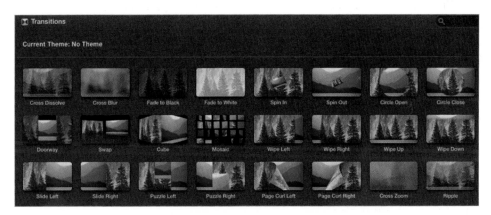

The browser fills with transitions. Because there is no theme in this movie, you see only the standard transitions.

2   Drag the Cross Dissolve transition between the clip of the door being locked (clip 7) and the first clip of the park (clip 8).

> **TIP** ▶ Transitions have a 1-second default duration. You can change the default transition duration by choosing Window > Movie Properties and then clicking the Settings button.

3 Skim to the start of the door being locked, and press the Spacebar to view the cross dissolve. Press Spacebar again to stop playback.

This is a good place for a transition from the black-and-white interior clips to the color clips of the outdoors, but first you'll explore some other transition options.

4 Select the transition in the timeline if it's not already selected. In the browser, skim the Circle Open transition to preview it in the viewing area.

5 Double-click the Circle Open transition to apply it to the selected transition in the timeline.

6 Skim to the start of the door being locked, and press the Spacebar to view the Circle Open transition.

The transition browser is very helpful for previewing transitions.

Changing Clip Playback Speed

Changing a clip's playback speed can enhance a dramatic or comedic situation; but, as with all jokes, it's funny once or twice and embarrassing if you use it all the time, so use it sparingly in your movies.

1   In the timeline, skim the first clip of Louisa playing in the snow.

This is already a fun clip, made more fun by splitting it into three parts. You can even give it more impact by speeding up Louisa's frolicking.

2   Click the clip to select it, and then choose Modify > Fast Forward > 4x.

This will make the clip play four times as fast as its normal speed. iMovie displays a rabbit icon on the clip to indicate the speed change.

3   Skim back before the speed change clip and press the Spacebar to review the speed change, and then press the Spacebar again to stop playback.

The second clip of Louisa playing in the snow needs the same speed change applied, but you'll apply it in a different way.

4   In the timeline, select the second clip of Louisa playing in the snow.

5   Control-click (or right-click) the clip, and choose Show Speed Editor from the short-cut menu.

The speed slider displays at the top of the clip.

6   Drag the speed slider to the left. The further you drag it, the shorter the clip gets, and the faster it will play.

NOTE ▸ Applying speed changes with the speed slider is useful when you want to set the speed based on where the clip will end in the timeline rather than on a specific speed value.

7   Skim back before the speed change clip and press the Spacebar to play the movie and review the speed change.

Now you have one last speed change to make: to speed up the last clip of Louisa traipsing in the snow. This time you'll do it the easy way.

8   In the timeline, select the clip of Louisa that you just applied the speed change to.

9   Choose Edit > Copy.

10   In the timeline, select the last clip of Louisa traipsing in the snow.

11   Choose Edit > Paste Adjustments > Speed.

The clip's speed changes to match the clip you copied from, and the filmstrip shortens in the timeline.

12   Skim back before the speed change clip and press the Spacebar to play the movie and review the speed change.

As you may have noticed, iMovie often provides more than one way to achieve the same result. Your method of choice may depend on how quickly you can get the result, the precision you desire, or merely which one pops into your head first.

Fixing Color Problems

Different video cameras use different color settings. Some cause skin tones to appear warmer, some increase color intensity, and some lose luster in low-light situations. Add to these variables fluctuations in filming conditions, such as different light sources or times of day, and you can see how easy it is to get very different-looking video in a single movie. Creating consistent color and brightness in your video clips makes for a visually more appealing movie. You don't want viewers to focus on the color variations between clips; you want them enjoying the movie. iMovie provides a number of controls to handle a range of color-balancing problems.

Enhance Video

The Enhance button in the toolbar is a one-click solution to instantly improve the look of your clips and improve the quality of the audio. If you're only aiming to improve one of those elements, you can use the Adjust button to be more specific.

1   Skim over the last clip in the timeline, with Louisa and the pink tutu on her head.

This clip has a few issues. It's dark and it also has a red tint to it.

2   Select the clip. In the toolbar, click the Adjust button.

3   In the adjustments bar, click the Color Balance button.

The Color Balance controls include buttons to correct skin tones, match color between two clips, as well as White Balance and an Auto button.

The Auto button in the Color Balance controls is almost identical to the Enhance button in the toolbar. The only difference is that the Enhance button also enhances audio.

4   Click the Auto button.

The clip instantly becomes brighter with a more natural color tint.

5   Click the Auto button to turn off the enhancement.

Now you're looking at the original color for this clip.

6   Click the Auto button again to reapply the enhancement.

Enhanced

That's the easy way out. It was completely automatic. It works pretty well most of the time, but on some clips you may want to make a more specific adjustment.

Adjusting White Balance

Your video camera has a setting called *white balance,* which essentially tells the camera if you're in sunlight or indoor light. Knowing this, the camera can correctly adjust for the different tints of color the different light types give off.

There's just one problem: humans! If you forget to set the white balance, you get blue-tinted images outside and orange images inside. That's why iMovie includes a white balance adjustment you can apply to your clips.

1   Skim the next-to-last clip in the timeline, with the two kids sitting outside.

Do you notice this clip has a decidedly bluish tint? You might conclude that their skin tone looks blue because they are freezing outside on a cold day, but that wouldn't explain the blue tint on the sidewalk or in Louisa's cap.

2   Select the clip. In the toolbar, click the Adjust button and the Color Balance controls if they're not already open from the previous exercise.

This time, instead of relying on automatic wizardry, you'll specifically correct the white balance.

3   Click the White Balance button, and then move the pointer over the clip.

The pointer changes to an eyedropper icon. Using the eyedropper you can correct the clip's white balance by selecting a part of the image that should be a neutral gray color.

4   Click the eyedropper on the right side of Louisa's white hat (your right, not hers).

The right side of the hat should be neutral gray since it is in the shade. When you click in the viewing area, the clip shifts to a warmer, less bluish tint. You can compare it to the original color by temporarily turning off the white balance adjustment.

5   Above the viewing area on the right, click the On button so it switches to Off.

Now you are looking at the original color for this clip.

6   Click the Off button so it switches back to On.

7   Click the checkmark in the upper-right corner to close the White Balance controls and accept the changes.

The effects you apply in iMovie are not permanent. Even though you changed clips to Black & White and shifted the white balance, you can return to wherever you made the adjustments and change them or remove them at any time.

Adjusting Skin Tone Balance

You can perform a type of color balancing similar to the white balance adjustment by using a person's skin tone. You'll end up with similar results where blue or orange tints are removed and colors are restored to normal.

1   Skim back to locate the clip of Louisa with chocolate on her face.

This clip has a pronounced pinkish tint, especially on the kids' skin.

2   Select the clip. In the adjustments bar, click the Color Balance button to open the Color Balance controls, if they're not already showing.

   This time, since Louisa is filling most of the frame and her face is what everyone will be staring at, that's what you want to look natural. You'll use the skin balance controls to get that fixed.

3   Click the Skin Tone Balance button, and then move the pointer over the clip.

   The pointer changes to an eyedropper. Instead of trying to find a neutral gray color as you did in the White Balance controls, here you'll look for a well-lit area of the face or arm.

4   Click the eyedropper on the right cheek (your right, not hers).

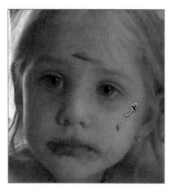

Clicking this cheek did tone down the pinkness, but only a little. You can keep click-ing different areas to get the results you want.

5   Click the arm on the right.

Since her arm had a much more saturated color, selecting it reduced the pinkish tint even more. Now you'll compare it with the original clip.

6   Above the viewing area, click the On button so it switches to Off.

Compared to the pronounced pink tint in the original clip, the skin tone looks more natural in the corrected version.

7   Click the Off button so it switches back to On.

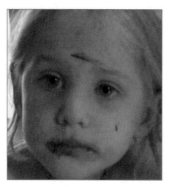

8   Click the checkmark in the upper-right corner to close the Skin Tone Balance controls and accept the changes.

Choosing to use the white balance or the skin tone balance to correct a clip depends on which issue is more prevalent in the clip, and how prevalent skin tones are in the viewing area. The clip where you did the white balance adjustment didn't have too much skin tone. In the clip you just fixed, Louisa's face and arms were clearly the focus.

Matching Color Between Clips

The last color balancing control is less about fixing something wrong with a clip's color and more about matching different clips so they appear consistent and from the same time and location.

1   Skim over the next-to-last and third-from-last clips in the timeline.

These two clips look very different, and having them back to back makes their color differences even more noticeable. The color of the last clip is much cleaner and more natural. Using the Match Color controls, you can make them appear much more similar.

Before applying this correction, make sure you set some expectations. You're not going to match the red from one clip to the red of another; this effect is not that specific. Rather, it looks at the color tint and brightness of two clips so that the overall appearance of one video clip aligns with the overall appearance of the other clip.

2   Select the third-from-last clip in the timeline. This is the clip you want to change.

3   Click the Match Color Balance button in the adjustments bar, and then move the pointer over the next-to-last clip in the timeline.

The viewing area now shows two clips. The one on the right is the clip you're going to change. The clip on the left is the color you want to match. You can skim to any clip in the timeline and any frame that best represents the overall color balance you want to match.

4   Click the eyedropper anywhere on the next-to-last clip in the timeline.

Unlike with the other color balancing effects, with color matching you don't click directly on the frame in the viewing area. You need only to click the filmstrip in the timeline.

When you do, the clip on the right brightens up and loses its yellowish tint.

5   Click the On button so it switches to Off.

Now you're looking at the original color for the clip on the right.

6   Click the Off button so it switches back to On.

7   Click the checkmark in the upper right to close the Match Color controls and accept the changes.

Those are three very powerful controls you can use very quickly to fix inconsistencies between clips. The results will yield a movie where viewers focus on the story you are telling and not on the visual inconsistencies between clips.

Stabilizing a Clip

When you shoot video without a tripod or monopod, you're going to wind up with shaky video. The iMovie Stabilization feature can help reduce and sometimes eliminate that video shake.

1   Play the fourth clip from the end of the timeline, showing Louisa walking with her dad.

Notice that the clip is shaking because the person with the camera is walking. This clip is a great candidate for stabilization because the camerawork is bumpy, but it's not totally erratic. Clips that move quickly from subject to subject are less likely to be good candidates for stabilization.

2   Click the shaky clip to select it.

3   In the adjustments bar, click the Stabilization button.

4   Select the Stabilize Shaky Video checkbox to begin the stabilization analysis. The activity indicator replaces the checkbox until the analysis is complete.

This analysis examines each frame and compares it to the frames before and after to calculate the camera movement. It's sophisticated stuff.

5   When the analysis is complete, press the Spacebar to play the stabilized clip. When you have finished watching the clip, click Done.

The stabilized clip plays back smoothly. You may also notice that the clip is slightly zoomed in. This is one of the side effects of stabilization: The shakier a clip is, the more it is zoomed to provide a little "elbow room" to perform the stabilization.

NOTE ▶ To adjust the amount of stabilization and the zoom-in factor applied to the clip, drag the Stabilize Shaky Video slider.

You can turn stabilization on and off to compare the results by selecting and deselecting the checkbox.

6   Deselect the Stabilize Shaky Video checkbox.

7   Play the clip to see the original shaky clip, and then select the checkbox and play the clip to see the stabilized results again.

Again you need to set some expectations for what this effect can and can't accomplish: Stabilization works best with a relatively stationary, clear subject in the clip but the camera is wobbly. Trying to stabilize clips of your kid playing soccer isn't going to work; your best bet for those situations is to use a tripod or hire a Hollywood camera man.

Working with Titles

To complete your movie, you need a title. You'll place a title at the end to accompany the music fading out.

1   In the Content Library section of the sidebar, select Titles.

Because you haven't applied a theme to this movie, the browser displays the standard titles.

2   Skim the pointer across the titles in the browser. A preview of each title animation is displayed in the viewing area.

3   Position the pointer over the Line title.

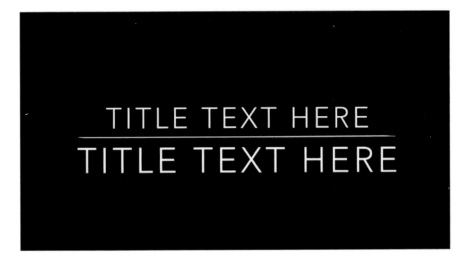

Unlike the Sports Theme title, most titles do not require you to place a color background for them to be applied. You can drag them anywhere in the timeline. If you drag them to an empty location in the timeline, the background will be black.

4   Drag the title to the end of the timeline, to the right of the last clip.

The purple title clip appears, previewing the location and duration of the title.

5   Release the mouse button to place the title as the last item in the timeline.

The last step is to change the text of the title.

The words "Title Text Here" are highlighted in yellow.

6 Type *A YEAR IN*, and then press Tab and type *NEW YORK CITY.*

7 Click in the timeline and skim just before the title.

8 Press the Spacebar to play the title.

With all the changes you made to this movie, you may have to trim the music to have it fit better.

Sharing Movies Online

With your movie complete, you can now share it with friends and family no matter where they are in the world. iMovie can upload to a number of popular web-based video sharing sites, including YouTube.

In this exercise you'll learn how to post to YouTube. (The other choices work in a similar way.)

Sharing to YouTube

YouTube is the most popular web destination for sharing video. It allows the world easy access to your movies. To share a movie, a trailer, or any other clip to any site from within iMovie, you begin by selecting what you want to share, and then clicking the Share button.

1 In the Libraries list, select "Max and Louisa in NYC."

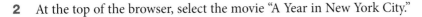

2   At the top of the browser, select the movie "A Year in New York City."

3   In the toolbar, click the Share button and choose YouTube from the pop-up menu.

The YouTube Share dialog appears with a few fields to fill in.

4   Enter a title if you want the title that appears on YouTube to be different from your movie's title.

5   Add any description and tags that will help YouTube viewers find your movie and understand what it is about before they view it.

6   Select the upload size of your movie. Larger sizes such as HD 720 or HD 1080 will create higher-quality video but will also take longer to upload.

7   Type in tags or keywords and select a category that best represents your movie, which will help people find your movie.

8   Choose who is allowed to view your movie:

▶   Private limits the viewing to you and the Google users you select. The movie won't appear on your YouTube channel or in search results.

▶ Unlisted makes the movie available to people you choose by sharing a link. These people do not need to have a Google account to see the video. Unlisted movies will also not appear on your YouTube channel or in search results.

▶ Public allows anyone to view your movie. It is posted on your YouTube channel and will show up in search results.

9   Click Next.

If this is your first time sharing to YouTube from iMovie, the Sign In dialog appears. You'll need to enter your YouTube account information to continue.

NOTE ▶ If you don't have a YouTube account, you need to create one at www.youtube.com.

10   Enter your account name and enter the account password, and then click OK.

NOTE ▶ Once you've entered your account name and password, you can change it in the future by using the Sign In button in the lower-left corner of the Share window.

11   After reading the YouTube Terms of Service, click the Publish button to upload your movie to YouTube.

Once the upload is complete, the Share Successful notification appears with a Visit button. Clicking the Visit button opens your web browser and loads the YouTube page with the movie.

12   To check to see if a movie has been published, select the movie in the browser.

TIP ▶ Shared movies cannot be removed from a website through iMovie. You must remove movies using the sharing service's website.

All the locations where the movie has been shared are displayed above the viewing area.

You can share your movies on other online sharing sites such as Facebook, Vimeo, and CNN iReport. The process is similar to sharing to YouTube. You can also remove your movies from a site by choosing Share > Remove from [site].

Lesson Review

1. How many effects can you apply to a clip from the effects thumbnails?

2. Where are transitions located?

3. Name one way you can modify clip speed once you've applied a speed change from the Modify menu.

4. What is the difference between the Enhance button and the Auto button found in the Color Balance controls?

5. Where are titles located?

6. What do titles look like in the timeline?

7. True or false? You can share only movies and trailers to YouTube.

Answers

1. Only one effect can be applied to a clip from the thumbnails.

2. Transitions are located in the content library.

3. Click the turtle or rabbit icon to display the Speed window, or Control-click the clip in the timeline and choose Show Speed Editors from the shortcut menu.

4. The Enhance button also works on audio.

5. Titles are located in the content library.

6. When you add titles to the timeline, they appear as purple bars.

7. False: You can select movies, trailers, or clips in the browser to share.

8

Lesson Files   Desktop > APTS iMovie Lesson Files > APTS iMovie Library > The Tiger's Nest

Desktop > APTS iMovie Lesson Files > Lesson 08

Time   This lesson takes approximately 150 minutes to complete.

Goals   Import photos

Find photos in a browser

Add a photo to a movie

Edit a cutaway

Add crossfades to a cutaway

Crop photos

Modify the Ken Burns effect

Freeze on a frame

Edit a title

Ducking background music

Lesson **8**

Making an Advanced Slideshow

Many of us shoot video with digital still cameras, iPhones, and iPads. Those clips usually sit side-by-side with photos taken at the same event. Most often you'll use iPhoto to show off photos and iMovie to show off video clips. It's high time to stop treating them like the green stuff on your dinner plate that you don't want touching the other food. You can easily mix clips from you iMovie library with photos from your iPhoto library or wherever they exist on your Mac to make spectacular-looking slideshows.

Accessing iPhoto

NOTE ► This first exercise is meant as an example only. The photos shown here are not intended to be identical to what you see in your iPhoto library. If you do not have iPhoto installed, you will still be able to complete the rest of this lesson, but for this first exercise you will only be able to read along.

Many video clips are captured using iPhones, iPads, and digital still cameras. If this is the case with your video clips, you can still access them directly inside iMovie and use them to make a movie.

1   In the Libraries list, select iPhoto Library.

TIP ► If you use Aperture instead of (or alongside) iPhoto, iMovie will also display Aperture in the Libraries list.

All your iPhoto events are shown in the browser. iMovie accesses them from your iPhoto library without moving them.

2   Select an event in the browser.

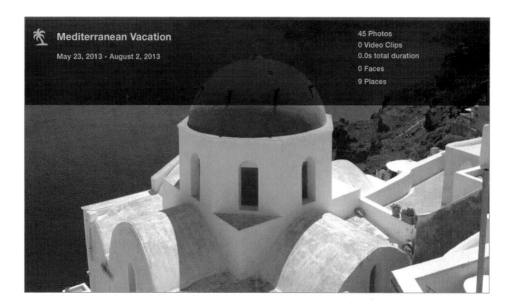

The event's representative key photo is displayed in the viewing area with information about the contents of the event.

3 From the pop-up menu above the browser, choose Albums or Smart Albums.

All the albums or Smart Albums you have created in iPhoto appear in the browser.

NOTE ▶ If you have not created any albums or Smart Albums in your personal iPhoto library, nothing will be displayed in the browser.

4 Double-click any album in the browser to view the photos in that album.

5 If you have a video clip in an iPhoto event or album, use the mouse pointer to skim over it, and then press the Spacebar to play the clip in the viewing area.

From the browser you are able to drag any photo or video clip into your timeline. But this is just one way of accessing your photos in iMovie. In the exercises that follow, you'll access photos directly from a folder on your desktop, and then you'll build a slideshow to music using those photos.

Importing Photos

If you don't use iPhoto or Aperture to organize your photos, you can import photos from any folder on your Mac just as you do video clips.

1   In the toolbar, click the Import button.

2   In the sidebar, select Desktop, and then navigate to APTS iMovie Lesson Files > Lesson 08.

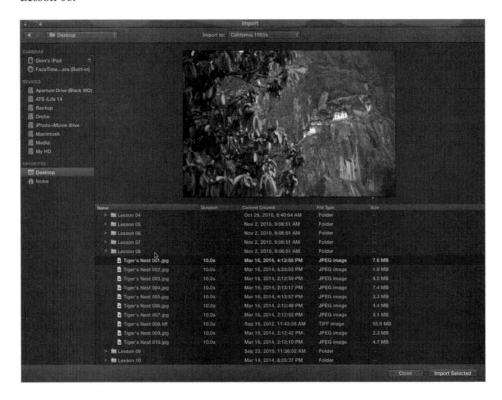

The contents of this folder are all photos. Clicking through any item in the lower half of the Import window shows the photos in the viewing area just as it does when importing video.

NOTE ▶ Photos you import into iMovie are kept in their native format and at their original size.

3 From the Import To pop-up menu, choose The Tiger's Nest event.

4 In the bottom half of the Import window, hold Shift and select the last Tiger's nest photo, Tiger's Nest 010.jpg. This selects all the photos in the Import window.

5. Cick Import All.

The photos appear in the browser as they continue to import.

Finding Photos in the Browser

Now you have all those beautiful photos in your browser mixed in with all those great video clips. This is great, but it poses a new problem: How do you find the photos without weeding through all the video clips?

1 At the top of the browser, type *photo* in the search field.

The photo browser filters out all the video and shows only photos. You can also search by name, or if you are using the iPhoto library, you can search on keywords, faces, or places.

2 Click the first photo in the browser to see it in the viewing area.

3 Choose View > Show Skimmer Info.

TIP ▶ You can enable skimmer info to view keywords assigned to clips from previous versions of iMovie. Clips with keywords will have a blue bar along the top.

4 Skim over a few photos in the browser.

The skimmer is helpful when you want to see the name of the clip or photo you are viewing.

5 To return to seeing all the contents in the browser, click the search field's Clear button.

Now you'll open the movie that you'll add these photos to.

6 At the top of the browser, double-click the "Climbing to the Tiger's Nest" movie to open it in the timeline.

The movie has the video clips and a title already in place that you'll use in your advanced slideshow. You need to fill it out using photos and music. But first watch it to see what you have.

7 Press the backslash (\) key to play the movie from the beginning.

You can have a lot of fun making these few clips into an exotic slideshow. You'll start by adding some photos.

Adding Photos to a Movie

Adding photos to a movie is similar to how you add video clips to a movie.

1   Choose View > Sort By > Name, and then choose View > Sort By > Ascending.

This places all those photos in the order in which you'll use them. You'll start with a scenic photo that shows the Tiger's Nest, which would make a better introduction than the current clip.

2   Scroll down the browser to find the photos.

3   Select the first photo in the browser and drag it to the left of the first clip in the timeline.

You can also insert photos between two clips.

4   Skim between the second and third video clips in the timeline until the skimmer snaps to the start of the third clip.

5   When the skimmer turns yellow, click to place the playhead at this location.

NOTE ▶ You can turn off snapping by choosing View > Snapping.

6 In the browser, select the second photo, and then Command-click the third photo.

7 To insert the two selected photos at the playhead location in the timeline, choose Edit > Insert from the shortcut menu.

You can use a replace edit to replace video clips with photos or vice versa.

8 Select the fourth photo in the browser.

9 Drag the photo onto the third clip from the end of the timeline. After the clip is highlighted white, release the photo.

10 From the pop-up menu, choose Replace.

11 Replace the next-to-last clip in the timeline using the fifth photo in the browser.

Photos added to the movie use the default 4-second duration. Your movie now has a basic structure in place. Play it from the beginning and see what you have.

Add a Cutaway

When you're making a movie, sometimes you decide to use a clip simply because it has good audio, even if the video is not so good. For those situations you can use what is called a cutaway.

1 At about the 35-second mark in the timeline, play the clip where the man talks about prayer wheels.

This is a fairly long clip of a man just standing and talking. We never actually get to see someone spin the wheel. It's perfect for a cutaway. While he continues to talk, the cutaway will show someone spinning the wheel up close.

To find a specific location in the clip for the cutaway, begin by using the Zoom slider in the Timeline to see more detail in the audio waveform.

2 Drag the Zoom slider about three notches from the right side.

3 Now with more detail showing in the timeline, skim towards the end of the clip when he begins to say "every time they spin the wheel."

4 Just before he says the words "every time," click the clip to position the playhead at this location.

This will be the start of the cutaway.

5 Type *video* in the browser search field to view just the video clips.

TIP If you've added keywords to clips in previous versions of iMovie, you can type in the search field to find clips that use those keywords.

6 In the browser, look for the video clip of the man spinning the prayer wheel.

7   Make a 4-second selection of this clip, and then choose Edit > Connect or press Q.

The cutaway is added above the main clips in your timeline.

8   In the timeline, skim prior to the cutaway clip and play the movie to preview your cutaway.

This cutaway works well to make that long clip more interesting. You can also use photos as cutaways.

9   Scroll the timeline to play the last video clip, where they reach the Tiger's Nest.

Most of this clip is good, but in the middle he explains that he'll tell viewers what's it's like inside, which he never does. Instead of teasing the audience, you'll remove that part of the clip. You want him to say "We are going to stop here for a minute," and then "Bye for now," removing everything in between.

10 Skim to where the man says, "We are going to stop here for a minute" (look for the "valley" in the waveform), and then click to set the playhead.

TIP ▶ When you're trying to locate exact audio locations, use audio skimming to hear the audio. If audio skimming is turned off, choose View > Audio Skimming to turn it on.

11 Control-click (or right-click) to view the shortcut menu.

12 Keeping the mouse pointer over the playhead, choose Split Clip.

Splitting a clip divides a single clip into two parts, making it easier for you to trim out the middle portion.

13 Skim over the clip to find the audio "Bye for now."

14 Just before he says the word "Bye," click to position the playhead.

Now you'll trim the clip from the split edit up to the location of the playhead.

15 Position the skimmer over the right edge of the split edit until you see the trim pointer.

16 Drag the right edge of the split edit to the playhead.

17 Skim back to the start of the last clip and press the Spacebar to review the edit.

The audio sounds OK, but the video has issues. Cutting out the middle of a clip creates what is called a *jump cut*, in which the camera position varies only a tiny bit between two adjacent clips. Jump cuts are usually considered bad (except in music videos, where they're considered edgy). One way to cover up a jump cut is to use a *cutaway*, in which you switch to another shot while the original audio continues. This time the cutaway will be a photo.

18 In the timeline, skim to the point in the last clip where he says "we made it to the top of the Tiger's Nest."

19 Click the timeline just after the words "Tiger's Nest" to place the playhead there.

This will be the start of the cutaway.

20 In the browser search field, clear the word "video" to view your photos again.

21 Click the sixth photo in the browser and press X.

22 Choose Edit > Connect or press Q.

23 Skim back to the start of the last clip and press the Spacebar to review the cutaway.

The cutaway is added above the main clips in your timeline. But it's not long enough to cover up the jump cut. You'll fix that by trimming the cutaway.

Trimming a Cutaway

The photo used as the last cutaway is too short. Photos are added into a timeline with a default 4-second duration, but the photo has no limit to how long it can be. So you'll trim out the photo to cover up the jump cut.

1   Position the pointer over the right edge of the cutaway clip until you see the trim pointer.

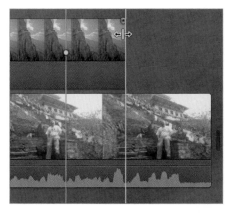

2   Trim the right edge of the clip to the right until it snaps to the edge of the clip below it.

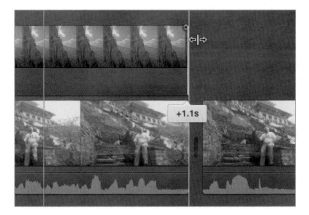

3   Skim back, and then press the Spacebar to watch the cutaway. Stop playing after the cutaway ends.

The cutaway ends perfectly, hiding the jump cut. You'll now add a few more cutaways to finish out the slideshow.

Moving a Cutaway

No matter how careful you are in placing the playhead when applying cutaways, you'll encounter situations when you need to move them.

1   Scroll the timeline just before the video cutaway of the man spinning the prayer wheel.

2   Stop playing just after the man spins the smaller prayer wheels in a clockwise direction.

The man talks about prayer wheels coming in different sizes. You will add cutaways that complement what he is talking about.

3   Type *photo* in the browser search field to view just the photos.

4   In the browser, Command-click the following three prayer wheel photos:

Two large prayer wheels

A row of small prayer wheels

Small handheld prayer wheel

5   Drag the three photos to the timeline, making sure they snap to the end of the video cutaway of the man spinning the prayer wheel.

> **TIP** ▸ You can turn Snapping on and off by choosing View > Snapping or pressing the N key on your keyboard.

Each photo has the default 4-second duration, which is very long. You can see in the timeline it completely covers up the man spinning the smaller prayer wheels, which is a nice clip.

6   Position the pointer over the right edge of the large prayer wheel photo until you see the trim pointer.

7   Drag the edge of the clip to the left until the help tag shows −2.0s.

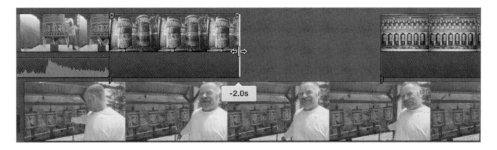

8   Trim the other two prayer wheel photos to also be 2 seconds.

Each prayer wheel photo is now the correct duration, but they need to be moved in the timeline so they are back to back.

9   Drag the second prayer wheel cutaway left until it snaps to the right edge of the first prayer wheel cutaway.

10   Drag the third prayer wheel cutaway left until it snaps to the right edge of the second prayer wheel cutaway.

You've assembled a smooth series of clips that show the movement and size ranges of prayer wheels using a sequence of cutaways. Play back the timeline to see how far you've come and then you'll learn a few more ways to improve your photo slideshow.

Adding Cross Dissolves to Cutaways

Up until now, your cutaways have been cuts. Although you cannot add a cross dissolve transition to a cutaway, you can fade cutaways with the clip they are placed over to make smoother transitions.

> **NOTE ▶** You cannot cross dissolve between two cutaways. A cutaway can only cross dissolve to the clip it is placed over in the timeline.

1   Scroll the timeline and play the first video clip in the timeline, of the man introducing viewers to the Tiger's Nest.

Once again this is a long clip of him talking. You can make it visually more interesting by including a photo of the picturesque Tiger's Nest.

2   Skim to the location in the timeline just before he says "and receive a blessing," and then click the clip to position the playhead at this location.

3 In the browser, select the last photo, and then choose Edit > Connect or press Q.

The 4-second photo is added as a cutaway at the end of the clip. You cannot add transitions from the content library to cutaways, but you can fade them in and out.

4 Drag the circular fade handle on either end of the photo in toward the center of the clip until the help tag shows +0.5s.

5 Press the backslash (\) key to watch the cutaway fade on and off.

At the end of the cutaway, you'll see a jarring pop from one video clip to another while the fade of the cutaway happens. To correct this you need to extend the length of the cutaway.

6 Place the pointer over the right edge of the cutaway clip until you see the trim pointer.

7 Trim the right edge of the clip to the right until the help tag shows about +0.5s.

8 Press the Spacebar to watch the cutaway. Stop playing after the cutaway ends.

The structure of the slideshow is in place. However, you may have noticed a slight pan and zoom added to every photo you placed in the timeline. This happens by default in iMovie. You'll leave the pan-and-zoom for some photos and remove it on others over the next few exercises.

Cropping Photos in the Viewing Area

By default, iMovie adds a pan-and-zoom movement called the Ken Burns effect to every photo placed in the timeline. While adding some movement on an otherwise static photo often looks nice, occasionally you need a static photo. One such situation is the first photo in the timeline, where you will eventually place the title.

1 Select the first photo in the timeline.

2   To see the Ken Burns effect on this photo, click the Play Selection button in the viewing area.

The Play Selection button plays only the selected portion of the timeline. It's very handy for reviewing effects, transitions, titles, and small areas of the timeline.

3   In the toolbar, click the Adjust button, and then click the Crop button to open the Crop controls.

The Crop controls are essential for photos, but they work on video clips as well. To remove the Ken Burns effect, you have two options: You can fit the entire photo in the viewing area, or crop the photo to fit into the viewing area.

4   Click the Fit button.

Most photos do not have the same *aspect ratio* as a video clip. This means their shape is different from the shape of a television screen. In order to fit a photo so the entire picture appears onscreen, padding must be added in the form of black filler on the sides of the photo. If it's critical to see the entire photo, this is the best choice.

5   Click the Crop to fill button.

The Crop to fill button adds a crop box to the viewing area that has the correct aspect ratio for a television screen. You can increase or decrease the rectangle to focus on an area of the photo you want but you cannot change the crop rectangle's shape. If you don't like having the black filler from the Fit setting and you can afford to lose outer parts of the picture, this is the best choice.

6   Drag the lower-left corner of the crop box in towards the center to remove some of the foliage on the left.

7 Position the crop box lower in the frame by dragging within the box.

8 Click the checkmark on the right side of the adjustments bar to accept the crop setting.

The Ken Burns effect is removed, and the crop setting frames the Tiger's Nest nicely for when you add the title over it.

Modifying the Ken Burns Effect

The Ken Burns effect never seems to get old and always looks great on photos. It is enabled by default when you add photos to a timeline, and you can modify its movement very easily.

> **NOTE ▶** Why is it called the Ken Burns effect? Ken Burns is a filmmaker famous for historical documentaries. Many of them use archival photographs, and to focus attention and create visual interest, he pans and zooms the camera on them.

1 Select the last photo cutaway in the timeline, and then click the Play Selection button in the viewing area.

You'll leave the Ken Burns effect on this photo but modify it so that it starts at the bottom of the photo and slowly pans up to see the Tiger's Nest. It will give a good sense of the tall, sheer cliff this monastery is built on.

2   In the adjustments bar, click the Crop tool.

NOTE ▸ Are you wondering why the Ken Burns effect is located in the Crop controls? It's because you're essentially resizing and positioning a starting crop frame and an ending crop frame that iMovie will animate between.

The yellow arrow shows the general direction the crop frame will move.

The start crop frame is the active frame when you enter the Ken Burns effect.

3   Drag anywhere within the start crop frame to position it so that the top line of the frame is at the bottom of the Tiger's Nest Monastery.

NOTE ► The Ken Burns effect randomly places the start and end frame differently for each photo, so you may not have to resize and reposition very much depending on the initial setting.

4   Click the end frame and drag to position it so the top line is just above the Tiger's Nest Monastery.

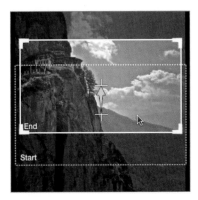

TIP ► The farther apart the start and end frames are, the faster the animation will move. To create slow, smooth motion, resize and reposition the frame in small amounts.

5   Click the checkmark on the right side of the adjustments bar to accept the Ken Burns setting.

6   Click the Play Selection button in the viewing area to see the results.

    If you ended up with a nice smooth pan up the cliff to end on the Tiger's Nest, you did a great job. If you didn't get that, try repositioning the start and end frames again so the yellow arrow in the viewing area points straight up. Then try another one.

7   Select the first photo cutaway in the timeline.

Instead of panning on this photo, you'll do a slow zoom in.

8 In the adjustments bar, click the Crop button.

9 Drag the lower-left corner so that it snaps to the left border of the photo, making sure to cut out any black fill on the left side.

10 Do the same for the lower-right corner, snapping it to the right border of the photo.

11 Drag up or down within the start frame to position it vertically centered in the photo.

12 Click the end frame.

The viewing area goes black because a fade is applied to the photo at the end. You can move the playhead back a few frames to see the photo prior to the fade beginning.

13 Press the Left Arrow key about a half-dozen times until you can see the photo.

NOTE ▶ You can move the crop frames without seeing the photo, but seeing the photo you are framing does help.

14 Drag the end frame so the upper-right corner lines up with the upper-right corner of the start frame.

15 Drag the lower-left corner in to make the end frame slightly smaller than the start frame.

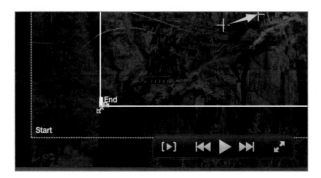

16 Click the checkmark on the right side of the adjustments bar to accept the Ken Burns setting.

17 Click the Play Selection button in the viewing area to see the results.

TIP ▶ You can click the Swap button to the right of the Ken Burns button to swap the start frame position with the end frame position.

The result is a beautiful, subtle zoom that draws the viewing area into the mysterious Tiger's Nest. For extra credit, try setting the Ken Burns effect on the three cutaway photos of the prayer wheel. Try different combination of pans and zooms.

Freezing on a Frame

Adding photos is one way to use a still frame in a movie; the other way is to freeze a frame from a clip.

1   Scroll the timeline to the last clip.

2   In the viewing area, click the Next button to ensure that the playhead is at the end of the timeline.

3   Press the Left Arrow key to move the playhead to the last frame of the last clip in the timeline.

4   Choose Modify > Add Freeze Frame or press Option-F.

5   Skim back to the cutaway and play the timeline to see the new freeze frame.

For some unknown and no good reason, iMovie creates the freeze frame and places it *before* the last clip. This makes no sense, so you need to move it *after* the last clip.

6   Drag the freeze frame to the right side of the last clip.

7   Skim back to the cutaway and play the timeline to see the new freeze frame.

That's a good last frame to end your movie on. Now you'll add a simple fade-out at the end using a crossfade, but instead of using the transitions from the browser, you'll use a quicker keyboard shortcut.

8   Position the playhead at the end of the freeze frame.

9   Press Command-T to add a crossfade transition at the playhead location.

That's a great way to end your movie and a much quicker way to add a crossfade than dragging it from the transitions in the browser.

Editing a Title

You've added titles previously in a few of the lessons. This time the title is already made but you're going to edit it to look nicer. You'll also reposition it over the photo at the start of the timeline.

1   Scroll to the start of the timeline.

2 Drag the title all the way to the left so it starts with the first photo in the timeline.

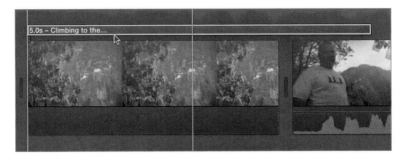

The title is longer than the photo, so you'll need to trim the title so it ends when the photo ends.

3 Place the pointer over the right edge of the title until you see the trim pointer.

4 Drag the right edge of the title to the left until it snaps in line with the right edge of the photo.

5 Press the backslash (\) key to view the movie. Press the Spacebar to stop once you have viewed the title.

The title is in place now, but it's not a very interesting title. First you'll replace this title with a new one and then you'll go on to style the text.

6 Click to select the title in the timeline.

7 In the Content Library section of the sidebar, select Titles.

8 From the browser, double-click the Horizontal Blur title to replace the existing title.

TIP ▶ Some titles contain different lines of text like subtitles and descriptions. Although you can replace all titles, using titles that have the same number of text lines works best.

9 Press the backslash (\) key to view the movie. Press the Spacebar to stop once you have viewed the title.

The title is updated with the new animation. Next you'll explore changing the text style.

Changing the Text Style

On some titles you can change the font, size, color, and alignment of the text so that it better fits with your movie.

1 Double-click the title in the timeline to open the adjustments bar with the title controls.

2 In the adjustments bar, choose Show Fonts from the Font menu.

Although you can choose a recently used font directly from the Font menu, the Fonts window will show you all the font options installed on your Mac.

3 In the Fonts window, select the All Fonts collection, Copperplate family, Light typeface, and 144 font size, and then close the Fonts window.

4 In the adjustments bar, click the Outline button to remove the black outline around the text.

Similar to a word processor, selecting a line, word, or even a letter allows you to customize the look of the selected characters.

5 Triple-click the Tiger's Nest line of text to select those two words.

6 In the adjustments bar, click the Bold button to make those two words bold.

7 In the adjustments bar, click the Color button and choose a bright buttercup yellow from the Color window, and then close the Color window.

8 On the far right of the adjustments bar, click the Apply button to close the title controls.

9 Press the backslash (\) key to play the title from the start of the movie. Press the Spacebar to stop after previewing the title.

You've got yourself a nice-looking title there. Well done. The last element to add is some mysterious music to complete your movie.

Ducking Music

Music is a significant part of every movie and yours is in need of it. You can use the royalty-free music supplied by iMovie and drop it into the background music track. The trick will be mixing it so it doesn't overpower the narration.

1   In the Content Library section of the sidebar, select Sound Effects.

2   From the pop-up menu at the top of the browser, choose Jingles.

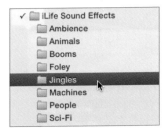

3   You can scroll the list of free music in the browser and preview different songs, but for this movie, scroll down to find Borealis.

4   Double-click Borealis to listen to it, and then click the Pause button to stop previewing.

TIP ▶ If you want to use only part of a song, you can drag out a selection in the music track that appears above the browser.

You'll add this to the background music track of your movie.

5   Choose Edit > Append to Background Music or press E.

6   Press the backslash (\) key to play the movie with the background music. Press the Spacebar to stop when you have heard enough.

That's a fantastic little movie you have there. It really catches the mystery of the Tiger's Nest, but the music overpowers the narration.

When you combine background music and dialogue, setting the audio at one level is often too limited. You would like the music to play loud when there is no narration and then get quieter when the person speaks. The easiest, and most automatic, way to mix narration and music like that is called *ducking*. Ducking automatically lowers all other audio tracks while a selected audio track plays in the timeline. When the selected audio track ends, the other audio tracks resume their regular volume.

7   Select the second clip in the timeline (the first time you see the man speaking).

8   In the adjustments bar, click the Volume button.

9 Select the "Lower volume of other clips" checkbox.

> With this option selected, iMovie reduces the music volume for the length of the selected clip. Then the music returns to its normal volume.

10 Play the timeline from the start.

> This sounds better. The music smoothly ramps down to a lower volume when the video clip begins. Now you'll do the same for the next narration clip.

11 To add another background music track where the first one ends, choose Edit > Append Background Music or press E.

> The same background music is added to the timeline, but it starts where the first music track ends. You need it to end at the end of the timeline.

12 Scroll to locate the clip of the man explaining prayer wheels.

13 Select the clip in the timeline, and then select the "Lower volume of other clips" checkbox in the adjustments bar.

14 Click the Play Selection button in the viewing area to play just the area you're interested in.

The music seems a little loud for his narration.

15 Drag the Ducking Volume slider slightly to the right to increase the amount of ducking, thereby lowering the music volume more.

16 Click the Play Selection button in the viewing area to play just the area you're interested in.

Sounding good. Your music ends way before the video, so you'll need to add the background music again so it can cover the end of the movie.

17 Choose Edit > Append to Background Music or press E.

18 Scroll to the end of the timeline.

19 Drag the new music track so its ending aligns with the end of the movie.

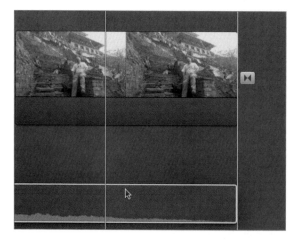

20 Now go through the timeline and select the "Lower volume of other clips" checkbox for each remaining clip in which the man speaks.

21 To view the complete movie in all its glory, place the playhead at the start of the timeline and click the Play Full Screen button in the viewing area.

Because you enabled ducking on the narration clips, the music ramps back up to its normal volume after the video clips end. Ducking makes it easy to achieve consistent results when mixing background music with other audio tracks.

Lesson Review

1. In iMovie, can you use photos that are saved in an iPhoto library?
2. If you didn't want a photo to have a Ken Burns effect on it, how do you remove the effect?
3. How do you view only photos in the browser?
4. How do you create a cutaway?
5. True or false? You can add cross dissolves to cutaways using the content library.
6. What is ducking?

Answers

1. Yes, iMovie accesses all the video clips and photos saved in your iPhoto library by selecting iPhoto library in the Libraries list.
2. If you want to remove the Ken Burns effect, you can choose the other cropping options, Fit and Crop to fill, in the Crop controls.
3. Enter *photos* in the search field above the browser.
4. Choose Edit > Connect or press Q.
5. False. You cannot add transitions from the content library to cutaways.
6. Ducking automatically lowers all other audio tracks while a selected audio track plays in the timeline. When the selected audio track ends, the other audio tracks resume their regular volume.

9

Lesson Files
Desktop > APTS iMovie Lesson Files > APTS iMovie Library > Glass Blowing

Time
This lesson takes approximately 70 minutes to complete.

Goals
Add maps to a movie

Use the precision editing view

Create a split screen

Get creative with color adjustments

Add a vignette

Paste multiple adjustments

Record a voiceover

Mix audio

Keyframe audio levels within a clip

Advanced Moviemaking

Is your creative appetite whet? Have the previous lessons been fun, but left you burning for something more? Maybe you're looking for ways to finesse your movie's story, or maybe you want to create something more visually intriguing. The editing features you'll explore in this lesson are aimed at assisting you in refining your storytelling, not just assembling your best clips and adding music and titles.

Choosing Projects from the Library

Once again, you'll begin by opening a movie that already has been started.

1 In the Libraries list, select All Projects.

Every project (trailers and movies) is listed as a thumbnail.

2 Double-click the Glass Blowing 101 movie to open it in the timeline and display it in the viewing area.

The Glass Blowing event is automatically selected to show the clips in the browser.

The movie demonstrates glass blowing. In this lesson, you'll finish this movie using some advanced iMovie features and sophisticated moviemaking techniques.

Setting a Location Using Travel Maps

The first question you face is how to start this movie. You've used various techniques and content including titles, photos, and movie clips; but one of the most engaging ways to start a movie is to show a map. iMovie maps can point out a single location or show a travel route for your vacation movie.

1   In the Content Library section of the sidebar, select Maps & Backgrounds.

The maps in the browser are broken down into three categories containing four styles each. The Globe and Map categories are the two that allow you to add travel lines and pinpoint locations.

2   Drag the Old World Map to the left of the first clip to make the map the first clip in the timeline.

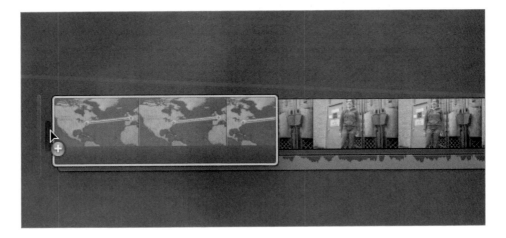

In this movie, you'll use the map to highlight Seattle, the location of the Pratt Center glass-blowing studio.

3   Click the map in the timeline. The map controls are shown in the toolbar.

4   Click the Start Location button, which currently is set to San Francisco.

5   In the search field, type *Seattle*. Three matching locations appear in the area below the field.

TIP Setting an end location will produce an animated line that travels from the start location to the destination when you play the movie.

6   Select the third entry, Seattle. The bottom of the window displays the text as it will appear on the map. You can customize the text to more specifically identify the location.

7   Click the word "Seattle" in the "Name to display on map" field.

8   Type *The Pratt Center, Seattle Wa.*, and then click Done.

The Pratt Center, Seattle Wa.

9   Press the backslash (\) key to review the result, and press the Spacebar to stop playback after you've seen the map.

Maps can add informative visual interest for educational videos, vacation movies, or even
videos for small businesses. If your movies don't take place in an iconic setting that's easily
recognizable in your clips, maps offer a great scene-setting alternative.

Trimming with the Precision Editor

The process of removing a few frames or seconds from clips in a timeline is called *trimming*. You did a bit of rough trimming in previous lessons, but now you'll employ a more
precise method. The precision editor is designed specifically for fine-tuning how one clip
ends and the next begins in your movie.

1   Press the backslash (\) key to play the movie.

2   Press the Spacebar to stop playback after the glass blower picks up the giant tweezers
(in the fourth clip in the timeline).

You may notice a few clips that need refinement.

3   Skim the third and fourth clips in which the glass blower sits down, and then examine
the close-up of her picking up the giant tweezers.

In the third clip, notice that she doesn't quite sit down, and then you cut to a long pause before you see her hand in the next clip. You can use the precision editor to improve the continuity of movement in these two clips.

4   Double-click the space between the third and fourth clip to open the precision editor.

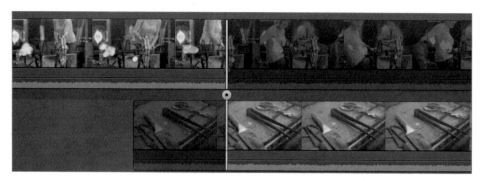

The precision editor opens in the timeline. It is a magnified view of the transition between the two clips. The white bar in the center indicates where the cut occurs between the third clip displayed in the top filmstrip (also called the *outgoing clip*) and the fourth clip displayed in the bottom filmstrip (called the *incoming clip*).

5   With your pointer positioned in the gray area under both filmstrips, skim back and forth to preview the transition.

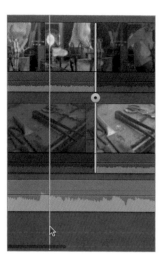

Skimming in the gray area below the precision editor is identical to skimming over the transition in the timeline. The skimmer extends over the top and bottom filmstrips to indicate it is showing both clips.

The filmstrip in the upper left of the precision editor shows the portion of the clip that plays before the transition, and the filmstrip in the lower right shows the clip that plays after the transition.

The shaded parts of the filmstrips, in the upper-right and lower-left areas of the clips, show portions of the clips that aren't used in the timeline.

6   Skim back and press the Spacebar to preview the current two clips.

The first thing you'll correct is the long delay before the hand enters the frame on the incoming clip.

7   Move the pointer over the white vertical bar on the bottom filmstrip.

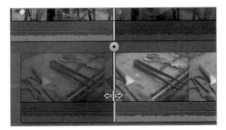

The pointer changes to a trim pointer.

8 Drag the white vertical bar slowly to the right until you see the glass blower's hand enter the frame, and then pick up a tool and leave the frame.

Dragging the white vertical bar is similar to trimming a clip. iMovie chooses a new starting point for the incoming clip.

9 With your pointer positioned in the gray area below the two filmstrips, skim back and then press the Spacebar to preview the new cut point.

You can refine the outgoing clip by extending it to include the glass blower sitting down and reaching for the tweezers.

10 Move the pointer over the white vertical bar on the top filmstrip.

The pointer changes to a trim pointer.

11 Drag the white vertical bar slowly to the right until you see the glass blower sit down and reach, being careful not to extend too far where she looks into the camera.

12 Skim back and press the Spacebar to preview the cut again.

You could have achieved the same results by selecting and deleting ranges, but the precision editor is a more adept refinement tool. It allows you to see the unused portions of each clip.

Trimming Audio in the Precision Editor

You can create more sophisticated transitions between clips by having video and audio content start at different times. Why would you want to do this? It can be a helpful way to hide content imperfections or to create a smoother flow through a transition.

1   While still in the precision editor, scroll the timeline back until you see the transition between the map and the first video clip.

2   Click the gray circle between the two clips to position the precision editor on these two clips.

You could improve a few things here. First, a long pause exists between the end of the map and when the glass blower speaks. If you attempt to trim out the pause before she speaks, the edit may seem very abrupt. In addition, the map just seems out of place without music or some audible introduction. By playing her audio greeting, "Welcome to Seattle," while the map is showing, and then switching to her video, you improve the transition and smooth the sequence of clips.

3   To make it easier to hear the words, choose View > Audio Skimming.

This enables audio while you skim.

4   Skim over the bottom filmstrip and stop just after the glass blower says "Welcome to Seattle."

You are now at the point where you want the cut to happen. Instead of dragging the white vertical bar and losing your current location, you'll drag the current location to the white vertical bar.

5   Drag the filmstrip to the left until your mouse pointer is under the white vertical bar (around –2.0 seconds).

You've now positioned the clip so that the first "welcome" sentence is cut off.

6   Skim back to the start of the map and press the Spacebar to confirm that you cannot hear "Welcome to Seattle" and that you can clearly hear her say, "The best thing to do here." If you trimmed too close to the next sentence (so that it sounds cut off), drag the filmstrip again where you think the clip should start.

7   In the precision editor, if necessary scroll the timeline up so you can see the blue audio track for the glass blower's introduction.

Here, you can trim the audio independently of its associated video.

8   Move the pointer over the blue audio waveform below the bottom filmstrip.

9   Skim near the white vertical bar until your pointer changes to a trim pointer.

10 Drag the white vertical bar the left, just before the glass blower says, "Welcome." Use the waveform to indentify where she begins to speak by dragging just to the left of the waveform peaks (a little over –1.0 seconds).

11 Skim back and press the Spacebar to preview the trimmed audio.

12 Click the Close Precision Editor button to return to the timeline.

You have created what is commonly called J-cut or split edit, a sophisticated edit that has connected the first two clips of your movie in a more fluid and polished manner.

You now have a beautiful looking movie but it doesn't really sound too good. So now you'll start working on the audio.

Recording Narration

In "how-to" movies such as the current one you're working on, it's helpful to include narration to help viewers understand what they are watching. You have three ways to record narration for your iMovie project:

▶   Record it at the same time you shoot the video.

▶   Record it with your Mac computer's built-in iSight camera.

▶   Record it using the iMovie Voiceover tool.

Recording Using the Voiceover Tool

The Voiceover tool allows you to record narration directly into your project. Your first step is to find the location in your project where you want to place narration.

1   Choose Edit > Deselect All to make sure nothing is selected in the timeline.

2   In the timeline, skim to the start of the third clip (counting the map), and then click to place the playhead at this location.

The narration line will be "First, we heat the glass." This third clip will fit nicely with that line so you'll start recording here.

3   Choose Window > Record Voiceover.

The Voiceover controls appear below the viewing area.

4   Practice saying the line of narration as if you were recording it. While practicing, watch the input meter in the Voiceover controls.

A good level primarily displays green, with yellow appearing only briefly during the loudest audio.

Red is bad. If you commonly see red displayed in the Voiceover controls, you need to decrease the input volume until the red no longer appears.

5   To decrease the input volume, click the Voiceover Options button to open the pop-up.

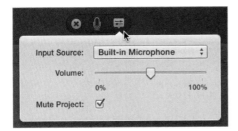

6   Drag the Volume slider left until you no longer see red while rehearsing the narration.

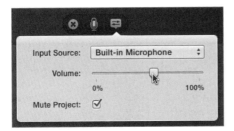

7   Click the Voiceover Options button again to close the pop-up.

8   Click the Record button to begin recording.

A 3-second countdown begins when you click the button, giving you a cue to begin speaking.

9 Press the Spacebar to stop recording.

10 If you aren't happy with your recording, select the new narration track that appears in the timeline and delete it. Then repeat steps 8 and 9 to try recording again.

11 Click the Close button to close the Voiceover controls.

12 Skim back over the second clip and press the Spacebar to listen to your new recording.

You now have your first voiceover track. The audio clip is also saved in the event so you can access it from the browser. Just like with any audio track in a timeline, you can move its location and change its volume level.

Using Audio from a Video Clip

In this next exercise, you'll use prerecorded video clips in the browser to add the second and third lines of narration.

1 At the top of the browser, play over the second clip of Taryn the glass blower, speaking into her iSight camera.

Taryn is speaking the second line of narration. You'll locate a good spot in your project to place this narration.

2   In the timeline, skim to the sixth clip and click in the middle of it to place the play-head at this location. This clip shows an assistant in the process of glass blowing.

3   Back in the browser, drag a selection range that encompasses Taryn's second line of narration.

4   Choose Edit > Connect or press Q.

This is a narration clip. Your viewers don't need to see her talking; for your movie you need only the audio. To remove the video but leave the audio from this narration clip, you must detach the two.

5   Select the cutaway you've edited into the timeline above the sixth clip.

6   Choose Modify > Detach Audio.

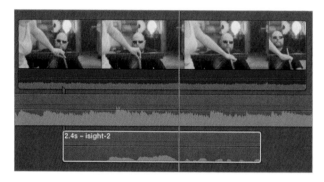

iMovie separates the audio from the video clip and places it under the main filmstrip.

7   Select the video portion of the cutaway and press Delete to remove it.

Only the audio from the clip remains. The green audio track can be moved, trimmed, and modified just like any audio track.

Mixing Audio

As you now know, placing the audio in your project is only the first part of working with it. You'll improve the audio mixing over the next few exercises using a few different audio tools.

Ducking, the Sequel

As you did in Lesson 8, you need to ensure that voices can be heard over music. Again, you'll use ducking to do this.

1   Play the timeline just before the second narration line and stop playback after the narration clip ends.

It's a very quiet narration compared to the music, so you'll duck the audio to lower the volume on both the video clip and the music.

2   Select the narration audio clip in the timeline, and then click the Adjustments button in the toolbar.

3   Click the Volume button, and then select the "Lower volume of other clips" checkbox.

4   Play the timeline to listen to the second narration track.

It's certainly better, but it's still quiet. Instead of using the timeline to adjust the volume, you can also do it in the volume controls.

5   Drag the Volume control slider to about 200%.

6   Play the timeline to listen to the increased narration volume.

You can also control how quiet the music becomes when the narration is playing.

7   Drag the "Lower volume of other clips" slider control slightly to the left.

The further left you drag the slider, the less ducking iMovie applies, and the louder the music volume remains.

8   Play the timeline to listen to the new mixed tracks of audio.

This mix is better. The volumes of the various tracks blend well together, but you can still make some improvements.

Equalizing Audio

Volume isn't the only control you have over audio. You can also apply equalization. Much like you control the bass and treble on your home audio system, you can use equalization presets to boost certain characteristics of audio tracks in iMovie.

1   With the second narration track still selected and the adjustments bar still displayed above the viewing area, click the Noise Reduction and Equalization button.

2   From the Equalizer pop-up menu, choose Voice Enhance.

3   Play the timeline to listen to the equalization-enhanced audio.

That's not bad, but it still sounds a bit muffled.

4   From the Equalizer pop-up menu, choose Treble Boost.

5   Play the timeline to listen to the equalization-enhanced audio.

That's much better. The narration is not only at a good volume, but it sounds brighter.

Keyframing Audio Levels Within a Clip

For more advanced mixing situations in which ducking the volume adjustment is too limiting, you can set varying volume levels within a single clip using the timeline volume control line.

1   Skim to the second clip in the timeline (the glass blower introduction).

This clip is too low since you pasted the audio level from the last clip earlier in this lesson. You'll raise the audio level first.

2   Move the pointer directly over the volume control line to see the volume pointer.

3   Drag the volume control line up until the help tag shows 100%.

Now the volume is at its default level.

However, the last half of the first clip is just wind noise and you've just increased it. Using equalization to remove the wind noise would make the glass blower's voice sound bad. Using the fade handles to fade out the audio will be too slow; it will still allow you to hear the first half of the wind noise. Your only real solution is to limit the wind noise by lowering the volume quickly in only that section of the clip.

4   Make sure audio skimming is still turned on from the View menu.

5   Move the pointer down over the clip's blue audio waveform and skim over the clip to locate the spot where she stops speaking, just when she starts to turn around.

> **TIP** You can turn waveforms on and off for timeline clips using the Thumbnail Appearance button.

The wind noise starts just as she turns, and this is where you want to begin to lower the volume level.

6   Move the pointer directly over the volume control line and you see the volume pointer.

This is where the audio begins to get quieter so you'll mark it with a keyframe.

7   Option-click the volume control line to set the keyframe.

Keyframes are markers you place in the audio waveform. They act as dividing points for setting various volume levels within a clip. You need at least two keyframes to change the volume level. One keyframe sets the louder audio level, and the other sets the lower volume level.

> **TIP** You may need to use the timeline Zoom slider to see more detail in the clip when setting keyframes.

8   Skim slightly to the right to find a location for your second keyframe, just before you hear any loud wind-noise pops.

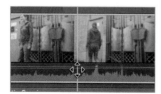

This second keyframe location determines how quickly the volume goes from loud to soft. You want to fairly quickly cut off the wind noise.

9   Option-click the volume control line just prior to any wind noise.

10 Drag the second keyframe down until the help tag shows about 10%.

11 Play the timeline to review the change, and then press the Spacebar to stop playback.

Changing the level has definitely reduced the wind noise and in a nice smooth way.

That's a much better transition from the voice level to the much quieter wind noise level. Next you'll do something about the background noise when she is talking.

Improving Sound Quality

You were able to improve the sound when no one was speaking by lowering the volume. That won't work in every case since verbal communication is an important part of most cultures. So you need to find ways to improve bad quality sound. Again, it's important to set expectations. If your audio wasn't recorded well, it won't ever be pristine in your movie. But you can improve it.

1   Select the second clip you've been working on, if it isn't still selected.

2   From the adjustments bar, click the Volume button, and then click Auto.

Clicking Auto in the Volume controls is the same as clicking the Enhance button in the toolbar. The only difference is that the Enhance button enhances audio and video, while the Auto button enhances only the audio.

The Auto button does a nice job of boosting the sound as much as it can without causing distortion. The problem with boosting the sound in almost every case (this one included) is that it also boosts the noise.

TIP You can turn off the automatic effect by clicking the Auto button again. When the Auto button is blue it is turned on; when it is white it is turned off.

3   To reduce the background noise, click the Noise Reduction and Equalizer button.

4   Select the "Reduce background noise" checkbox.

5   Play the clip in the timeline to listen to the noise reduction.

The default setting does a decent job of keeping her voice clear while removing the background noise. You can adjust the slider for the background noise to see if you can achieve better results. Dragging the slider left lets more noise in, but also makes her voice sound more natural. Dragging the slider right further reduces the background noise, but also causes her words to be clipped off.

6   Drag the background noise slider to see where you prefer the setting.

7   Deselect the "Reduce background noise" checkbox to listen to the original clip audio, and then reselect it to hear your adjustment.

To fill in tones of her voice that the noise reduction may have removed, you can try different equalizer presets.

8   Choose Voice Enhance from the Equalizer menu.

This was the obvious preset to choose, but without even playing the clip you can tell it caused a lot of distortion. When the tips of the audio waveform show red, the audio is too loud and it is distorting. You want the very tips of the waveform to show that mustardy yellow color, but never red.

TIP You can use the Thumbnail Appearance button in the upper-right corner of the timeline to show the Clip Size slider. Increasing the timeline clip sizes will help you see (and correct) the red distortion more easily.

9   To fix this distortion, place the pointer over the volume control line. When the pointer changes to the volume pointer, drag the line down to remove the red in the waveform.

10   Play the clip in the timeline to listen to the equalizer setting.

You can try different equalizer presets to see which you prefer. Always notice how the equalizer changes the waveform. More than likely, you'll have to adjust the volume control line each time you choose a new preset. Always set the volume control line so the loudest part of your audio is displayed in the mustard yellow color and not the red.

Lesson Review

1. Where do you find maps in iMovie?
2. What does the top filmstrip in the precision editor represent?
3. How do you start recording a voiceover?
4. Where can you see all the projects created in your library?
5. Name one of three methods you can use to improve sound quality.
6. How do make audio a separate track from its video?

Answers

1. In Maps & Backgrounds in the content library
2. The top clip represents the first clip in the transition, also called the outgoing clip.
3. Choose Window > Record Voiceover, click the location in the timeline where you want the recording to be placed, and then click the Record button.
4. In All Projects in the Libraries list
5. The Equalizer presets, the Reduce Background Noise option, or the Auto button
6. Choose Modify > Detach Audio.

10

Lesson Files   None

Time   This lesson takes approximately 35 minutes to complete.

Goals   Understand video formats

Adjust a clip's date and time

Consolidate event media

Back up your library

Move events and projects

Managing Your Library

Now that you have a firm grasp of how to use iMovie to make fantastic movies, it's time to turn your eye toward the fundamentals of managing the video in your library. iMovie not only captures clips from different devices; it also helps keep them in a neat and orderly library. Since this lesson goes over how to manage multiple libraries across multiple hard drives, not every reader will be able to follow the step-by-step instructions. Still, it's worth reading to get a better understanding of how iMovie manages your library.

Understanding Video Formats

Transferring video from a camcorder or an iOS device to your Mac computer's hard disk using iMovie follows a very similar process to the one you learned in Lesson 2. Although the process is standard, video formats themselves can vary widely. To better understand how to make videos, you need to understand video formats first.

Sizing Up Standard and High Definition

Almost all video recording devices for sale over the past five years record in high definition (HD) with options to record in standard definition (SD). It's similar to an HD television set that can still show the SD stations. Simply put, HD video provides a larger frame size with a more detailed, sharper image than SD video. You've probably noticed the difference when switching between clear HD stations that fill up your TV screen and the somewhat fuzzier SD stations that typically have black pillars along the side. iMovie works seamlessly with both SD and HD video formats, and you can even use them both in a single project, almost without ever even realizing it.

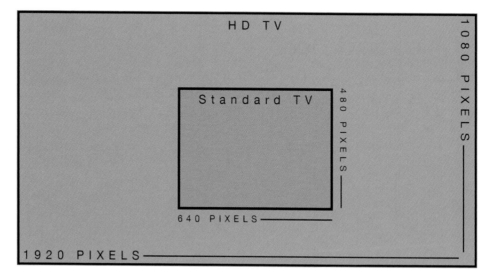

HD video is 1920 x 1080 pixels. SD video is 640 x 480. Because HD video contains more pixels, it requires more hard disk storage space and faster hard disk performance.

Learning About Aspect Ratios

HD and SD have different frame shapes, or *aspect ratios*. HD's widescreen aspect ratio is 16:9 (16 by 9), like all modern flat-screen TVs. SD's squarer aspect ratio is 4:3 (four by three), the familiar shape of the older tube television sets that you see sitting outside on the curb with the "free" sign on them. iMovie handles switching between different aspect ratios without a hitch.

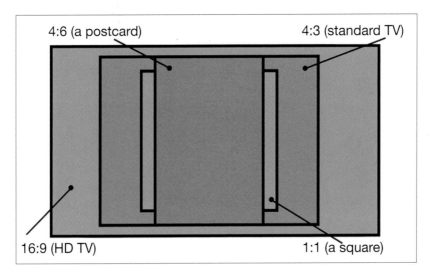

Commonly used aspect ratios

Learning About File Types

Video is recorded in a wide variety of file types, including AVCHD, M4V, MOV, and many others. Each video recording device compresses the video in different ways in order to make it small enough to fit on a memory card or in your iOS device's internal memory. iMovie stores all the files "natively" in the library, which means the files are not converted once they come off the device they were recorded on. This ensures the original quality of the video clips is retained once they get inside iMovie. The different compression formats used by different recording devices are transparent once they are imported.

Handling SD and HD in the Same Project

As facile as iMovie makes working with different video formats, with all these different frame sizes and aspect ratios, some situations create challenges you should be aware of.

The first clip you add to a new movie or trailer determines your new project's size.

1   In the Libraries list, select California 1950s.

These clips are SD-sized clips (640 x 480). You can tell by the viewing area's almost square aspect ratio.

2   In the toolbar, click the Create button, choose Movie, and then create a movie using the No Theme setting.

3   Name the movie *SD Movie* and click OK in the dialog.

4   Add any clip from the California 1950s event into the new movie.

The viewing area has now changed to a 16:9 aspect ratio.

If the clips in the browser are SD clips with a 4:3 aspect ratio, why does iMovie use a 16:9 aspect ratio? It's even more curious because I specifically said iMovie determines the new project frame size based on the first clip you add.

The answer is, I lied… partially. iMovie uses the first clip you add to the timeline to decide between two project frame sizes: the larger 1920 x 1080 HD size and the smaller 1280 x 720 HD size. iMovie never makes projects smaller than 1280 x 720.

5   Scroll to the top of the browser and select the SD Movie project.

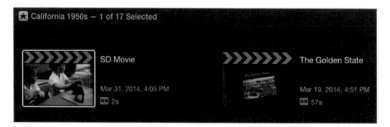

Above the viewing area the project size says 720. This is shorthand for 1280 x 720, about half the size of 1920 x 1080 HD.

Only when you add a 1920 x 1080 clip as the first clip in a new project does iMovie use the much larger 1920 x 1080 project frame size.

So why, when you see a 640 x 480 video like the California 1950s footage in the iMovie 1280 x 720 frame, don't you see those black bars (pillars) on the side of the viewing area? The next steps show what iMovie has done.

6   In the timeline select the clip and click the Adjustment button.

In the adjustments bar, the Crop button is highlighted as if you cropped the clip, but of course you didn't. iMovie does this automatically for SD clips edited into a project.

7   Click the Crop button.

Now you see the pillars along the sides of the clip. You also see the crop box used to crop the SD clip to fit into the 16:9 aspect ratio. This is good to know when you use an SD clip in a movie and iMovie crops the head off the top of the frame. You need to use the Crop controls to reframe the crop box.

8   Click the Accept button on the far right of the adjustments bar to close the Crop tools.

Mystery solved. iMovie uses two HD project sizes, and it chooses which project size to create based on the first clip you add to the timeline. When you add an SD clip to a project, iMovie crops and scales the SD clip to fit into the HD project frame.

Adjusting a Clip's Date and Time

If the date was set incorrectly on your camcorder, or—as with the California 1950s event—for some reason, your clips have incorrect date information, you can enter or modify the dates for every clip.

> **NOTE ▶** If you have not completed Lesson 2, import the Old Home Movies folder from Desktop > APTS iMovie Lesson Files > Lesson 02 in order to follow these steps.

1   Select the California 1950s event, if necessary.

2   Choose View > Show Separate Days in Events.

The date for the clips is displayed in each event. The California 1950s event shows March 2014. But these clips were filmed throughout 1958. The 2014 date reflects when the movie files were created on disk.

3   Select the first nine clips in the library, which were taken on June 25, 1958.

All 9 clips are selected and you can now change their creation dates.

4   Choose Modify > Adjust Clip Date and Time.

A window displays the time and date of the first clip. The other clips will be offset based on how you set the first clip.

5   In the To field, change 3/11/2014 to *6/25/1958*.

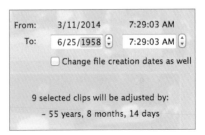

6   Click OK.

7   If necessary, click the Glass Blowing event and then back on the California 1950s event to update the browser.

The event now correctly shows that the selected clips are dated June 25, 1958. As you can see, the event's remaining clips are still in a time warp in March 2014, so feel free to change their date to 1958.

Making Backups

As your library grows, you'll have more and more important memories stored in various events. You really should be backing up your projects and events to another hard disk. With digital files, one hard disk failure can wipe out all your clips and video memories.

Consolidating Media

This first thing you have to do before you start making backups is to figure out all your file locations. Collecting your events and their associated movies or trailers in one location will make creating backups much easier.

If any of the video clips, music, and other media used in a movie are stored on a hard disk other than the one that contains the movie itself, you can collect the files onto the same disk as the project.

1   In the All Projects category of the Libraries list, select a movie or trailer.

2   Choose File > Consolidate Project Media.

The dialog explains that iMovie will copy the files used in the project to the drive where the project resides.

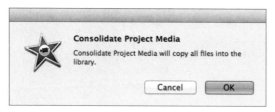

TIP iTunes songs used in the project are copied to the same disk as the project once you edit them into the project. If you move the disk to another Mac, some iTunes songs may need to be authorized to play on that Mac.

3   Click OK.

If the video files and the project file are all located on the same disk, iMovie displays a dialog explaining that nothing needed to be copied. After consolidation, the project will reference the video files in its new locations on the project disk. Consolidating doesn't inherently make a backup, but it does collect all your media into one location, thereby simplifying the process of copying everything to a backup drive.

Copying Libraries

Maybe the easiest way to back up a library is just to copy it from the Movies folder of your hard drive onto an external hard drive.

1 Quit iMovie.

2 In the Mac OS X Finder, locate your Movies folder.

By default, iMovie creates your first library in the Movies folder. Assuming you have only one iMovie library and you haven't created others, this library contains all your events, video files, movies, and trailers.

3 To create a backup copy, drag iMovie Library onto an external hard drive.

4 Once the library is copied, rename the new library on the external hard drive as *iMovie Library Backup*.

This is the easiest way to create a backup, but it's also the most time consuming. After you make the first copy this way, you need only to copy the new events and projects added since you created the backup. So let's look at how you can back up individual events and projects.

Moving Events to an External Hard Disk

With your events and projects consolidated into one location, and a full library backup created, you can easily move just new events to the backup drive from within iMovie. You can move a single event or a project. You'll start by moving an event because it's so easy.

TIP ▶ To create a library on an external hard drive, choose File > Open Library > New. Then name the library and save it to the external hard drive.

1   In the Libraries list, select an event.

2   Choose File > Move Event to Library.

3   From the submenu, choose the library where you want to move the event.

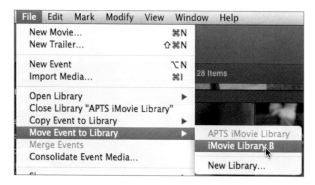

TIP ▶ Moving an event to a new library on a different hard drive removes it from the current library. If you want to place the event on a different hard drive but also leave it in the current library, choose File > Copy Event to Library.

The event and all its clips (even rejected clips) are moved into the library on the external hard drive.

Moving Projects to an External Hard Disk

Moving events moves the projects in the event and every clip in the event. You can also move a project with only the clips that are used in the project.

1   Select a project in an event.

2   Choose File > Move Project to Library.

3   From the submenu, choose the library where you want to move the project.

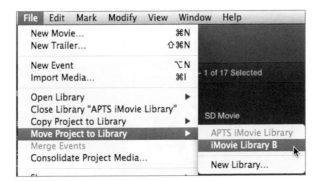

TIP > Moving a project to a new library on a different hard drive removes it from the current library. If you want to place the project on a different hard drive but also leave it in the current library, choose File > Copy Project to Library.

The project is moved to the new library and removed from the original library. The clips used in the project are copied to the new location. All the clips still reside in the original library.

Bonus Lesson: iMovie Theater for Mac

A bonus lesson is your next step in completing the iPhoto for Mac lessons. You've already learned how to share your projects to popular social networks. The bonus lesson expands on sharing by covering iMovie Theater on the Mac. iMovie Theater is a library of all the movies and trailers you've made and uses iCloud to automatically share them to all your devices, even your Apple TV.

For those using the eBook, you'll find all Bonus lessons after the index. For those using the printed book, you can access the Bonus lesson online.

To access the iMovie Mac OS Bonus lesson:

1   Connect to the Internet, and navigate to www.peachpit.com/redeem, and enter your access code.

2   Click Redeem Code, and sign in or create a Peachpit.com account.

3   Locate the iMovie Mac OS Bonus lesson on your Account Page under the Lessons & Update Files tab.

4   Click the iMovie Mac OS Bonus link and download it to your Downloads folder.

5   After downloading the file, open your Downloads folder, and double-click iMovie Mac OS Bonus.zip to unzip it.

The iMovie Mac OS Bonus lesson is provided in PDF form and uses the same lesson files you've been using throughout this book.

Lesson Review

1. True or false? If you select a single clip in an event and adjust its date or time, all other clips will change based on the new date or time of the selected clip.

2. If the first clip you add to a new movie is 1920 x 1080 pixels, what frame size will the project use?

3. Is Consolidate the best way to copy clips and projects to an external drive?

Answers

1. False. Only selected clips are changed. If you want to change the date and/or time of all clips, you must select all clips.

2. The project will create a 1920 x 1080 project frame size.

3. No. Consolidate only moves or copies clips or events to the same disk as the project. The best way to copy a project along with its event and clips is to choose File > Copy Event to Library.

iMovie for iOS

11

Lesson Files	None
Time	This lesson takes approximately 55 minutes to complete.
Goals	Understand iMovie for iOS
	Browse and skim clips
	Tag your favorites
	Change the filmstrip display
	Share a clip to Facebook

Learning the Fundamentals of iMovie for iOS

Welcome to iMovie for iOS. You're probably skeptical that all the great things you just learned about iMovie for Mac could be squished down to fit into your iPad screen, let alone your iPhone. I was too. I wondered, even if they could fit it all onto an iOS device, why would I want to use it when I can use iMovie on my big Mac screen? Then I realized the extraordinary fun of sharing a clip or making a hilarious movie trailer spontaneously. The reason to use iMovie on your iOS device is that it's always in your pocket whenever you want it.

The following lessons take you through iMovie for iOS. They use many of the same video clips from the earlier lessons. Even so, it's not recommended that you copy the clips onto your iOS device. Unlike your Mac, your iOS device doesn't have a lot of memory for you to copy extra video clips onto it. However, these lessons are designed for you to follow along with the step-by-step instructions using your own clips.

Understanding iMovie for iOS

When you record a video clip on your iPhone or iPad, it is saved in the Photos app that comes with iOS 7. If you've recorded any video to your iOS 7 device, you have video clips in iMovie because iMovie has access to all the video clips (and photos) in the Photos app.

> **TIP**▸ If iMovie isn't installed on your iOS 7 device, you can download it from the App Store.

The moment you record a video clip on your iOS device, it shows up in iMovie. There's no import or saving from one place to another. It's just there. Of course, recording a video clip using the iOS device's camera isn't the only way to get a video into iMovie.

iMovie for iOS uses video clips from three sources:

▸ Videos captured with the iOS 7 camera or saved from an email or text message (and in some cases other apps), which show up in the iMovie video browser

▸ Video clips you record using the camera built into the iMovie project view

▸ Video clips synced from iPhoto on Mac OS X through iTunes

> **NOTE**▸ The example screens in this guide are taken on an iPad in landscape mode (that is, with the Home button on the left or right side). When the iMovie screen on the iPad differs significantly from an iPhone, both devices are shown.

To view your video clips, begin by launching iMovie.

1   In the iOS Home screen, tap iMovie.

When you open iMovie for the first time, you'll see the welcome screen with an outline displayed to help you get started with iMovie.

2   Tap Continue.

NOTE ▸ If you've previously opened iMovie, this note may not appear and you may already have an iMovie library with personal video clips stored in it.

The iMovie app has three main screens. Each screen is accessed by tapping a button at the top of the screen.

3   Tap Video.

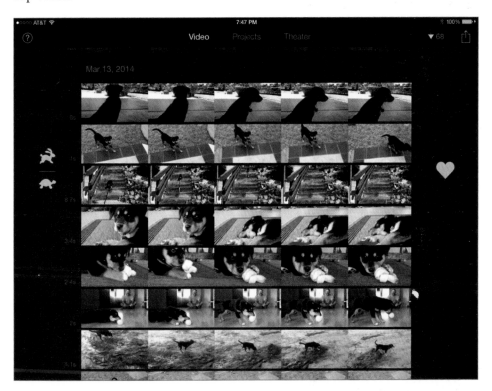

The video browser shows all the clips from the Photos app, recorded with the built-in iMovie camera or synced from iPhoto for Mac. The clips are grouped in chronological order by month.

4 Tap Projects.

The projects view shows movies and trailers you have created in iMovie for iOS.

5 Tap Theater.

iMovie Theater is a central location for all your completed projects.

If you're new to iMovie for iOS, you may have clips only in the video browser. The other two views may be empty. Still, you can have a lot of fun just browsing, viewing, and sharing clips.

Browsing and Playing Clips

Once you have video clips in the video browser, they are displayed as filmstrips. Filmstrips are created using multiple representative frames, called thumbnails. Using the filmstrips, you can quickly see and jump to any portion of any clip.

1   Tap Video to view the video browser.

2   In the browser, swipe up and down to view all the clips in the browser.

3   Tap any filmstrip to open the viewing area.

4   Drag over the filmstrip to quickly preview the clip in the viewing area.

5   Tap the Play button to play the clip.

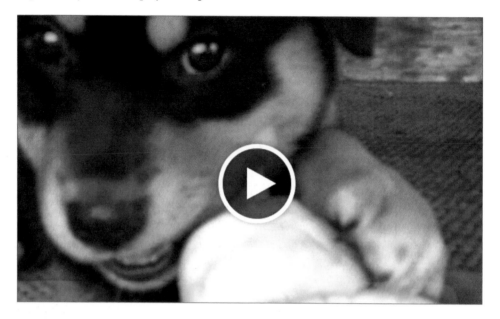

6   Tap anywhere in the viewing area to stop playing.

If you want to preview a clip quickly, you can fast forward it.

7   Tap a different filmstrip to open the viewing area.

8   Tap the Fast button ![rabbit icon] to play the clip at 2x normal speed.

9 Tap the Fast button again to play the clip at normal speed.

10 Tap anywhere in the viewing area to stop playback.

If you want to slowly preview a clip, you can play a clip at half speed.

11 Tap any filmstrip to open the viewing area.

12 Tap the Slow button  to play the clip at half normal speed.

13 Tap the Slow button again to play the clip at normal speed.

14 Tap anywhere in the viewing area to stop playback.

Browsing and playing are a good beginning technique, but you use a few other techniques to more easily find the best parts of your clips.

Tagging Your Favorite Clips

Sometimes an entire clip is filled with feel-good moments, and sometimes just a few seconds are worth viewing. iMovie provides a simple tool for tagging, so you can quickly find and view the best parts of each clip.

Tagging Favorites and Selecting a Range

Video clips in your browser fall into two categories: those you love and those you love slightly less. For the clips you love, iMovie includes a quick way to tag them as favorites.

1   Tap a filmstrip in the browser to open the viewing area.

A yellow selection outline surrounds the filmstrip, indicating the range within the clip that will be tagged as a favorite.

If you love the entire clip, you can tag it as a favorite.

2   Tap the Favorite button .

The green line at the bottom of the clip identifies it as a favorite.

The clips you love slightly less are probably very good in parts. For those clips, you can select a clip range to tag as a favorite.

3   Tap a filmstrip in the browser to open the viewing area and show the yellow selection outline on the filmstrip.

You can narrow the selection range by dragging the handles on the yellow selection outline.

4   Drag the handle from the left side of the filmstrip in towards the center of the film-strip until your favorite part begins.

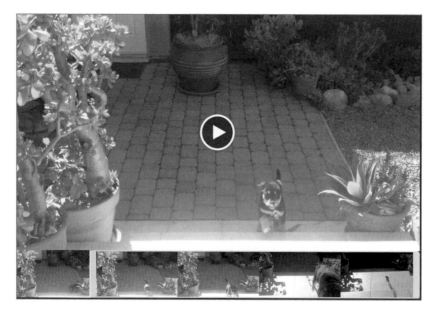

The viewing area updates for you to see the exact frame you are dragging over.

5   Drag the handle from the right side of the filmstrip in towards the center of the filmstrip until the end of your favorite part.

6   Tap the Favorite button.

A green line appears from the start of the yellow selection outline to the end of it.

Clearing a Favorite Tag

If a clip falls out of favor and is no longer a favorite, you can clear the favorite tag from the clip.

1   Tap a filmstrip in the browser to open the viewing area.

The yellow selection outline surrounds the filmstrip.

2   Tap the Favorite button.

The green line is removed from the filmstrip, and the clip is no longer considered a favorite.

Changing the Filmstrip Display

You can change which filmstrips appear in the browser, and the order in which they are displayed.

1   At the top of the video browser, tap the disclosure triangle.

2   Tap Oldest First.

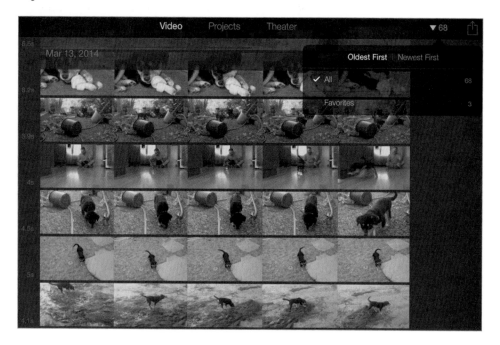

3   On the iPhone, tap Done to hide the menu.

The order of filmstrips is reversed with the oldest clips at the top of the video browser. You can also limit which filmstrips are displayed.

4 On the iPhone, tap the disclosure triangle to open the menu again.

5 Tap Favorites, then, on the iPhone, tap Done.

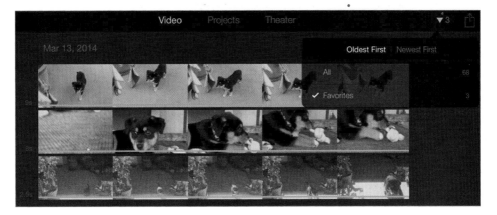

Only the clips or portions of clips tagged as favorites are shown in the browser.

6 From the disclosure triangle menu, tap All.

7 On the iPhone, tap Done.

All the tagged and untagged filmstrips are back in the video browser.

Sharing Clips to Facebook

Facebook has over 1 billion members. Chances are you or some of your friends and family members are on there already. And you, or people you know, have probably shared video clips. You can easily share your favorite clips to Facebook as well as other popular video sharing sites, or through email and text messages. The process is similar for all the sharing sites, so you'll learn how to share to Facebook, which will give you a good idea how to share to the other sites.

NOTE ▶ This exercise assumes you have a Facebook account and a Wi-Fi or cellular network connection to the Internet.

1 From the video browser, tap the filmstrip for a clip you would like to share online.

2   Drag the yellow handles to select the clip portion you want to share.

3   At the top of the video browser, tap the Share button .

The Share popover opens showing the different sharing options, including YouTube, email, and text messages.

4   Tap Facebook.

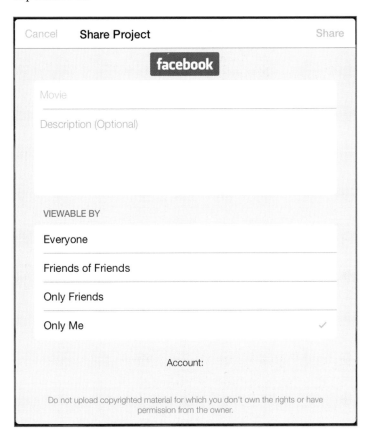

NOTE ▶ If you are not signed in to Facebook on your iOS device, you will be prompted to sign in at this point.

In the Facebook window, you can name the video clip, give a description that will show on Facebook, and select a Viewable By option to determine who is allowed to see the clip.

5   In the Facebook window, name the clip, add a description of the clip, and tap Only Friends so that only your "friends" on Facebook can view the video clip.

6   Tap Share at the top of the window when you have finished entering the information.

The dialog that appears offers a link to your Facebook page to view the clip online.

Lesson Review

1.   What are the three main screens in iMovie?

2.   True or false? Tapping the Play button twice will cause a clip to play back faster.

3.   How do you tag only a portion of a clip as a favorite?

4.   What does the disclosure triangle at the top of the screen in the video browser do?

5.   What is this button used for?

Answers

1. Video, Projects, and Theater

2. False. Tapping the Fast button will cause the clip to play back faster. Tapping the Fast button again will return it to normal speed.

3. Tap the filmstrip, drag the yellow handles to define the portion of the clip, and then tap the Favorite button.

4. The disclosure triangle displays a popover where you can change the display order for filmstrips and filter the video browser to show only favorite clips.

5. The Share button is used to share clips from the browser to popular web sharing sites, through email, or via a text message.

12

Lesson Files	None
Time	This lesson takes approximately 45 minutes to complete.
Goals	Pick a trailer genre
	Edit a trailer outline
	Fill in a storyboard
	Change clips in a trailer
	Personalize a storyline

de Rejected

ing to the Tiger's Nest — 1m 22s

30.0s   34.1s

Producing a One-Minute Movie

Creating an iMovie trailer is the effortless way to produce hilarious one-minute movies. *Trailer* is a term used in Hollywood to describe the coming attractions you see before a feature presentation. After capturing a few clips on your iOS device, instead of just posting them on Facebook, drop them into one of the movie genre templates and you've got yourself a bigger-than-life, Hollywood-style coming attraction.

These lessons are designed so you can follow the step-by-step instructions using your own videos.

Picking a Trailer Genre

Trailers and movies are the two types of projects you create in iMovie. You begin making a project by switching to the project view.

NOTE ▶ The example screens in this guide are taken on an iPad in landscape mode (with the Home button on the left or right side). When the iMovie screen on the iPad differs significantly from an iPhone, both devices are shown.

1   In the video browser, tap Projects at the top of the screen.

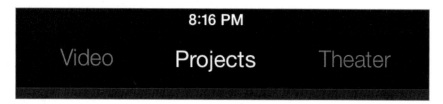

The project view is an empty screen to start with, but each project you create will be displayed here.

2   To create a project, tap the Create button ➕ at the top of the screen.

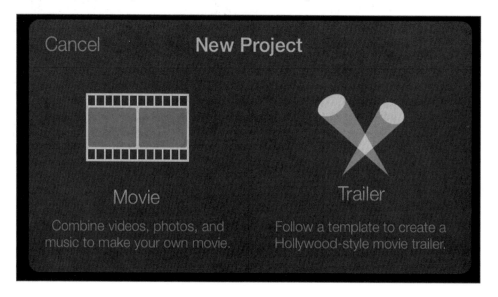

You can choose between creating a trailer or a movie.

3   Tap Trailer.

These trailer templates represent different movie genres, such as action, horror, adventure, and sci-fi. Don't worry if you don't have clips that were recorded to be used in these types of movies. You'll be surprised how well your birthday party, family gathering, or weekend ski trip clips work in these trailer templates.

4   Swipe through the different trailer genres.

iPad

iPhone

5   When you come to a trailer you're interested in, tap the Play button to preview it.

6   Tap the Pause button to stop playing.

Each template shows the eventual trailer duration on the right side and the number of "cast members" the trailer focuses on in the lower left. If no cast members are listed, any number of people can appear in the trailer.

7   After you decide on a trailer, tap Create Trailer.

The trailer view appears.

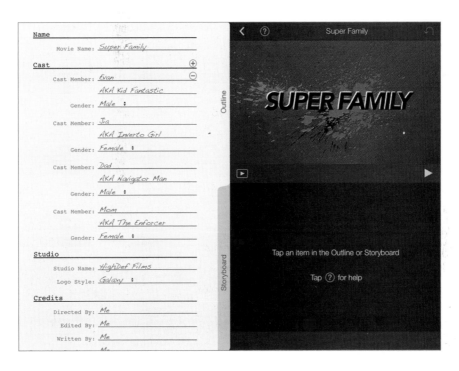

On the iPad, the left side of the screen shows the outline and storyboard that will guide you through adding your clips and customizing the story outline. The right side of the screen contains the viewing area and an area where you can select clips.

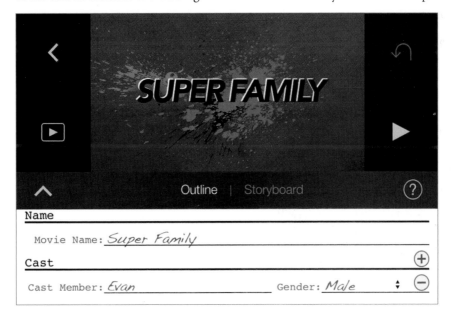

On the iPhone the top half of the screen is the viewing area, and the bottom half shows the outline and storyboard. Your clips will be displayed as needed.

Edit the Outline

The outline is where you can personalize the title, cast members, studio name, and credits for your trailer. You'll start by changing the title of the trailer.

NOTE ▸ Trailers with no specific number of cast members mentioned on the New Trailer screen will not have any cast members to customize.

1   On the Movie Name line, tap the existing title, delete it, and enter the title of your movie trailer. Tap Done.

The new title is displayed in the viewing area just as it will appear in the trailer.

Now you can move on to the cast members.

Some trailers allow you to add and delete the number of cast members in the trailer. If there are no cast members in your trailer, move on to edit the studio logo.

2   To delete a cast member from a trailer, tap the Remove button ⊖ .

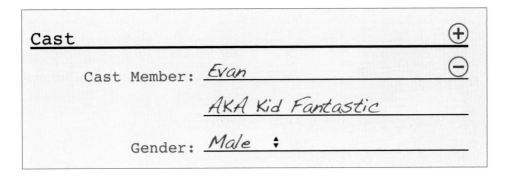

You can customize remaining cast members to represent friends or family members.

3 Tap a cast member name and remove the existing text, and then type in the name of a friend or family member who will be in the trailer.

4 Tap Gender and match it to your first cast member.

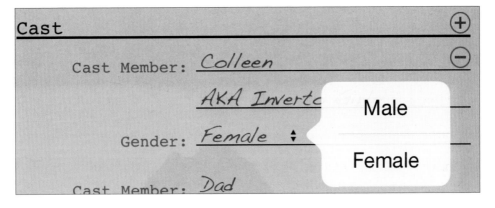

The Gender setting is used so that pronouns in the trailer titles match the cast members you add.

5 When you've finished removing and adding cast members, tap the studio name.

The studio logo is displayed in the viewing area referencing famous studio logos.

You can choose the name of the studio and which studio logo you want in the studio fields. Changing all of these fields is not necessary but adds to the fun of the trailer when you play it for friends and family.

6 Tap the Studio Name field and enter your customized name.

7   To change the studio logo, tap the name next to Logo Style.

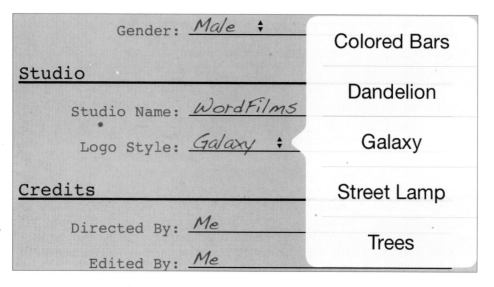

A popover shows the studio logo choices.

8   Tap any studio logo to see it in the viewing area.

9 To play the logo, tap the Play button in the lower-right corner of the viewing area.

10 Tap the Pause button after the logo is finished and the trailer starts.

11 In the Outline pane, swipe up to view the trailer credits.

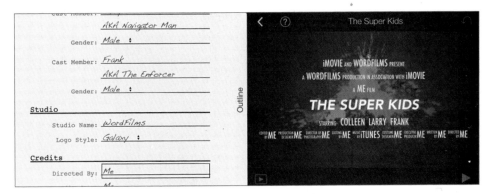

12 Tap the Directed By field to see the credits in the viewing area.

By default, iMovie fills in the credit list using the My Card setting in the address book of your iOS device, but you can change each credit as necessary. You can fill those credits in at your leisure; for now you'll move on to adding clips.

Filling in the Storyboard

With the outline personalized, you can start creating the storyboard.

1 Tap the Storyboard tab.

iPhone

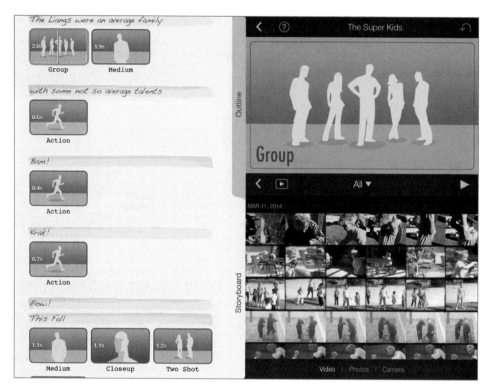

iPad

The storyboard placeholders describe the types of clips to add, how long those clips should be, and an appropriate order for the clips. You'll start by playing the trailer without adding any clips to get a sense of what you are filling in.

2   Tap the Play button to play the trailer.

The trailer includes titles, music, and all the placeholders you need to create a complete coming attraction. All you need to do is select the clips to match the placeholder descriptions.

3   Halfway through the trailer, tap the Pause button to stop.

The viewing area jumps back to the first placeholder. In the storyboard, the first placeholder is highlighted blue to give you an indication of the type of clip you need to find.

4   On the iPhone, tap the first placeholder in the storyboard to open the browser.

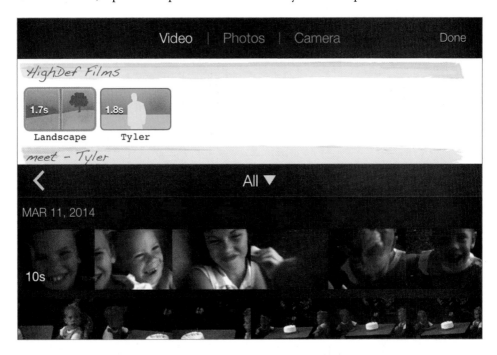

5   In the browser, tap any clip that matches the first placeholder description.

A yellow selection highlight appears on the filmstrip, giving you an indication of how much of the clip will be used to fill in the placeholder.

6 Tap the Play button under the selected range to preview the portion that will be added to the trailer.

7 Tap the arrow button  to fill in the trailer placeholder with the selected range.

The placeholder is filled in with the selected clip, and the blue highlight moves to the second placeholder in the storyboard as shown in the viewing area.

8 In the browser, tap any clip that matches the placeholder description.

If your initial selection isn't exactly what you want, you can tap a different filmstrip or refine the current selection.

9 To choose a different range from the same clip, drag the yellow selection range to a new area on the filmstrip.

You don't have to worry about the size of the selection range since the placeholder determines how long the selection must be. You need to be concerned only with where the selection starts.

10 When you have filled in all the placeholders, do the following:

▶ On the iPad, tap the Play Full Screen button ▶ to play the trailer full screen from the beginning.

▶ On the iPhone, tap Done in the upper-right corner of the screen, and tap the Play Full Screen button ▶ to play the trailer full screen from the beginning.

Now you know how to create trailers by replacing placeholders using clips from the browser. But if you want to ensure that you record all the clips needed for a trailer, you can record them live using an iOS device's camera.

Recording Directly to a Trailer

Each placeholder in the trailer's storyboard tells you the type of clip that works best at that point. You can even use the built-in camera on your iOS device to record clips directly into the placeholders. So instead of capturing a bunch of random clips at a party, or during a vacation, you can follow the trailer's storyboard and you'll end up with a fantastic home video.

1 While viewing the trailer storyboard, tap the placeholder you want to fill in.

You can tap any placeholder and fill it either using the clips from the browser or with video that you record live with the iOS camera.

2 To open the camera, do the following:

▶ On the iPad, at the bottom of the browser, tap Camera.

iPad

▶ On the iPhone, above the storyboard, tap Camera.

iPhone

The viewing area is replaced with the camera's live view.

On the iPad, the browser is replaced with the placeholder you will be filling in.

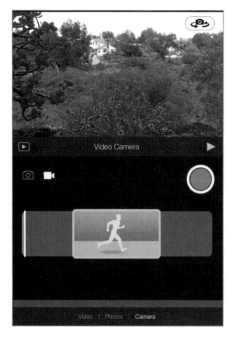

3 Tap the Record button to begin recording the clip for the placeholder.

4 When the recording is done, tap Video to return to the video browser.

> **TIP** ▶ You can tap the Photos button under the camera's live view to use a photo to fill in the placeholder.

iMovie records 4 seconds more than what the placeholder requires, including a 3-second countdown. When the required duration of the placeholder is recorded, the recording stops and the clip is added to the trailer.

Changing Clips in a Trailer

In some cases you may want to replace one clip in the trailer with a different one from the browser.

1 In the storyboard, tap the clip you want to replace.

The clip appears in the viewing area. Under it is the filmstrip for the clip.

2 Tap the Trash icon 🗑 to remove the clip from the trailer.

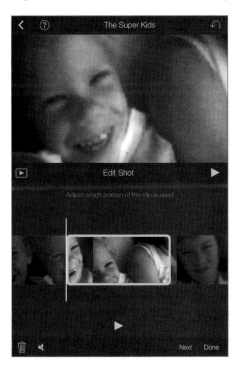

The clip is removed from the trailer but remains in your browser.

3   Tap the placeholder in the storyboard to select it.

The browser shows all the clips you can use in the trailer.

4   Tap the disclosure triangle above the browser.

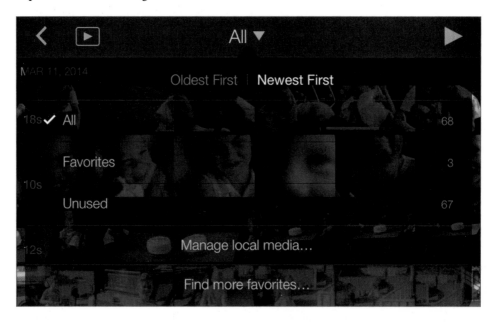

The popover that appears is similar to the one you used in Lesson 11 to filter clips, with a few additional items for trailers and movies.

5   Tap Unused. To close the menu on the iPad tap the disclosure triangle again. On the iPhone tap Done.

The browser is now filtered to show only clips that have not been used in this trailer.

6   Tap a filmstrip, then tap the insert arrow to add the clip to the selected placeholder.

7   Tap the disclosure triangle, and then tap All.

Knowing that you can change your trailer even after all the placeholders are filled relieves the creative pressure when you're producing your first cinematic masterpiece.

Using the Edit Shot Pane

More often than changing an entire clip, you will probably want to adjust the part of the clip you are using in the trailer. You can do that using the Edit Shot pane.

1   In the storyboard, tap a clip you want to adjust.

When the action you're trying to capture in the clip falls outside the portion used in the trailer, you can use the Edit Shot pane to shift the selection range.

2   Drag the filmstrip right or left in the Edit Shot pane to shift the selected range earlier or later in the clip.

As you drag the filmstrip, the viewing area shows the first frame from this clip that you will use in the trailer.

> **TIP** By default a clip's audio is set to mute in a trailer. You can enable audio for a clip by tapping the audio icon in the Edit Shot pane.

3   Tap the Play button in the Edit Shot pane to view the new selected range.

4   If you want to adjust the next clip in the trailer, tap Next.

5   When you have finished adjusting clips, tap Done.

The trailer is complete, and you can play it to review what you've created. It's a delightful movie to watch, but you could still improve it.

Personalizing the Storyline

One way to start improving your trailer is to edit its titles. The stock titles provided by Apple are a good starting point but customizing them will make the trailer more personal.

1   Swipe to the top of the storyboard.

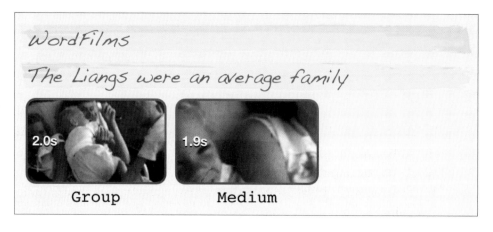

Titles appear as blue bars throughout the storyboard.

2   In the storyboard tap a blue bar you would like to change.

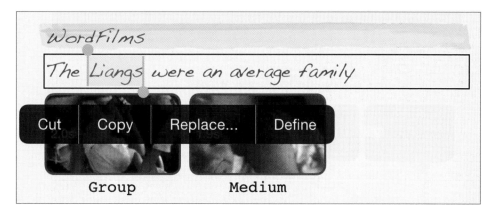

Depending on the title, some words may be split into different text boxes.

3   Tap Clear in the center right of the screen to remove all the text, or tap a word, and then tap Select from the popover and type a new word.

4   Tap Done when you have finished typing.

> **TIP** ▶ Tap Revert next to the Clear button if you want to undo your changes and restore the original text.

After you make the changes, you can play the trailer to see the entire movie.

5   To play the trailer full screen, do the following:

▶   On the iPad, tap the Play Full Screen button to play the trailer full screen from the beginning.

▶   On the iPhone, first tap the collapse button ▼ to reveal the viewing area, and then tap the Play Full Screen button to play the trailer full screen from the beginning.

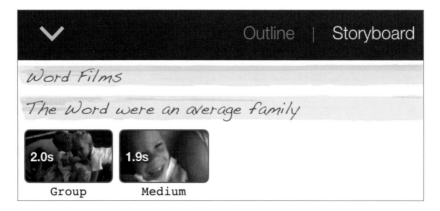

Trailers offer a unique way to show off your video clips in style. And just like the movie you made in the previous lesson, you can share it to Facebook or to another social network supported in iMovie.

Lesson Review

1. Where do you find the choices for movie trailers?
2. How can you change the studio logo at the beginning of the movie trailer?
3. What determines the length of a clip added to the trailer?
4. True or false? Once you add a clip to a trailer you cannot change it.
5. True or false? You can change the trailer style at any time while you are making the trailer.

Answers

1. View the movie trailer genres by tapping Create and choosing Trailer.

2. After you create a new trailer, you can select a studio logo from the Outline tab.

3. A clip's length is determined by the placeholder in the trailer.

4. False. You can change a clip in the trailer by tapping the Undo button and tapping another clip in the browser.

5. False. Once you begin creating a trailer, you must start over again if you want to select a new trailer style.

13

Lesson Files	None
Time	This lesson takes approximately 100 minutes to complete.
Goals	Start a new movie
	Use the playhead
	Rearrange clips in a movie
	Add and adjust audio
	Apply titles and transitions
	Switch themes
	Use photos in a movie
	Master advanced movie-making options
	Save and move projects
	Delete clips and projects

Mobilize Your Movie Making

Mobile movie-making is growing in popularity all over the world. You can capture amazing HD video on your iPhone, start to edit the clips on the spot, then transfer your movie onto your larger iPad screen and finish making the movie there. In this lesson, you'll graduate from filling in the blanks with trailers to assembling clips in your own way. You'll lose the structure of the trailers, but that doesn't mean you have to sacrifice their polished look. Movie projects have their own special polish and a lot more flexibility.

These lessons are designed so you can follow the step-by-step instructions using your own videos.

Starting a New Movie

In iMovie, you create a movie project similar to how you start creating a trailer. Selecting a theme for a movie is like selecting a genre for your trailer. But you have other decisions to make: the length of your clips, the placement of transitions, and the soundtrack for your movie.

> **NOTE** ▶ The example screens in this guide are taken on an iPad in landscape mode (with the Home button on the left or right side). When the iMovie screen on the iPad differs significantly from an iPhone, both devices are shown.

1   In the video browser, tap Projects at the top of the screen.

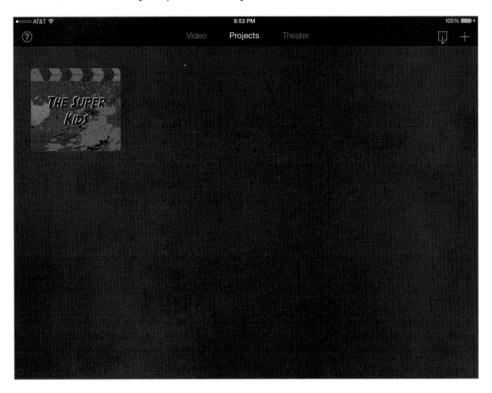

The project view shows trailers you've already created. It's also the place where you create movie projects.

2   To create a new project, tap the Add button 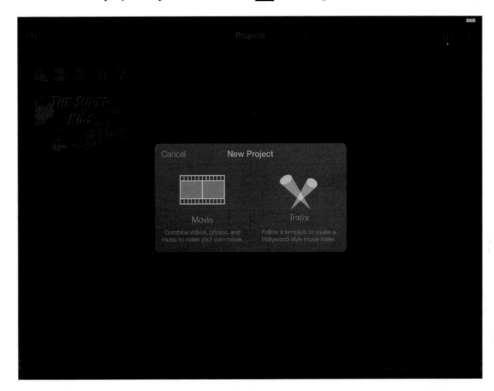 at the top of the screen.

In this dialog you can choose to create a new trailer or a movie.

3   Tap Movie.

iPad

iPhone

You can choose among different looks or themes for your movie. The themes are based on design styles such as neon, playful, and modern. They define how the titles and transitions look as well as the default music.

4 Swipe through the different themes to find one you like.

5 When you come to a theme you're interested in, tap the Play button to preview it.

6 Tap the Pause button to stop playing.

7 To choose a theme, tap Create Movie.

The project view that opens appears slightly different on an iPad and iPhone.

The iPad has three main areas:

▶ Viewing area: Where you watch your movie and clips

▶ Media library: Where you select clips, photos, and music to add to your movie

▶ Timeline: Shows each clip in your movie, laid out in the order they appear

Viewing area   Media library

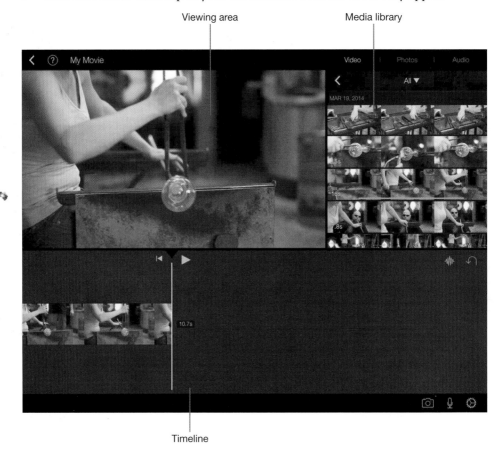

Timeline

The iPhone has two main areas:

▶ The viewing area is where you watch your movie and clips.

▶ The bottom half switches between the timeline and the media library.

Viewing area

Timeline (or media library)

Similar to adding clips to a trailer, to add clips to a movie you select the best parts of your videos and add them to the timeline.

The difference between selecting clips for a trailer and selecting clips for a movie is that the trailer already has defined lengths for each clip you add. In a movie, you decide the length of the selection to add.

8 To select clips you want to add to the timeline, do the following:

► On the iPad, swipe up and down in the media browser to view all the clips.

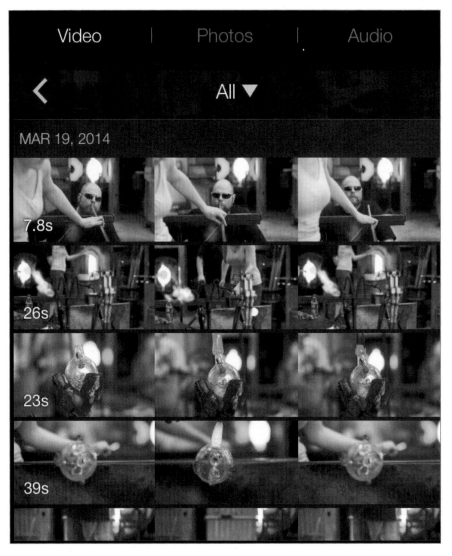

▶   On the iPhone, tap the Media Browser button  to view the clips in the browser.

9   Tap any filmstrip to select it and open the popover.

10   Drag over the filmstrip to quickly preview the clip in the viewing area.

11   Tap the Play button in the popover to play the clip.

12   Tap anywhere on the filmstrip to stop playing.

13   Drag the yellow handles from the left and right side of the filmstrip to select the range you want to add to the movie.

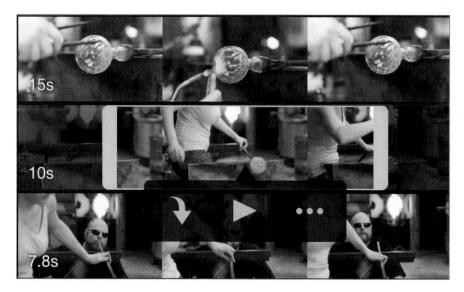

14 From the popover, tap the arrow button  to add the selection to your movie.

iMovie places the clip in the timeline. An orange line appears at the bottom of the filmstrip in the browser, indicating the portion of the clip that is used in the movie.

15 Return to the browser, select a range, and tap the arrow button to add another clip to the timeline.

The clip is added to the end of the clip in the timeline. The gray box between the two clips in the timeline represents a cross-dissolve transition added automatically by iMovie.

Using the Playhead

You learned in the last exercise that tapping the arrow button places a clip after the last clip in the timeline. But that's not the whole story. What happens when you want to add a clip to the beginning of the timeline?

1 Drag the timeline filmstrip to the right until the playhead (white line) is at the start of the movie.

The playhead shows you the current position in the timeline based on the current frame in the viewing area.

2   Return to the browser and tap any filmstrip to select a clip and open the popover.

3   Tap the arrow button to add the selection to the timeline.

This time, the clip is added to the beginning of the timeline instead of the end. The location of the playhead determines where the clip will be added.

TIP You can use the disclosure arrow at the top of the browser to view and add only your favorite clips to the movie.

4   Drag the timeline filmstrip until the playhead is roughly centered over a clip.

5   Tap any filmstrip in the browser to select a clip and open the popover.

6   Tap the arrow button to add the selection to the timeline.

TIP Tap the Undo button below the browser on the iPad or to the right of the viewing area on the iPhone, to undo your last action.

Where iMovie adds the selection depends on where you placed the playhead. In a general sense, if the playhead is even slightly off-center, the selection will be added to the side of the clip the playhead is closer to. So if you want a clip to be added before a clip in the timeline, position the playhead so it is closer to the start of the clip.

Rearranging Clips in a Movie

On many occasions, you'll have the right clips in your timeline, but in the wrong locations. You can rearrange clips to place them in the best storytelling order.

1   In the timeline, tap and hold a clip you want to move.

This clip pops up from its position in the timeline.

2   Drag the clip to a new position in the timeline.

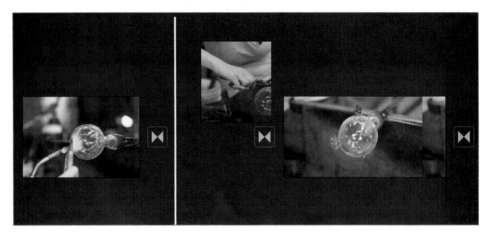

When you drag a clip in the timeline, the other clips shift to make room, giving you an indication of where the clip will land when you release it.

3   When your finger is located where you want to place the clip, raise your finger from the screen.

The clip drops into place.

Don't be afraid to try different clip arrangements. You can always move a clip back to its original position by tapping Undo below the browser on the iPad or to the right of the viewing area on the iPhone.

Adding and Adjusting Audio

Music plays a large part in setting the mood for your movie. iMovie comes with royalty-free background music tracks selected specifically for each theme. All you have to do is turn it on.

1   While viewing the timeline and viewing area in the project view, tap the Project Settings button 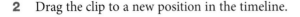.

TIP On the iPhone, if you are viewing the browser, you can return to the timeline and viewing area by tapping Cancel in the upper-right corner of the screen.

The Project Settings window displays themes and preferences for your movie.

2   Tap Theme Music to turn on the background music track that accompanies the theme you chose when you created the movie.

3   On the iPad, tap the Project Settings button again to hide the settings. On the iPhone, tap Done in the upper right.

A green line representing the background music track is added to the timeline. Depending on the length of your movie, the background music track loops to fit the length.

4   Swipe the timeline back to the start of the movie, and then tap the Play button under the viewing area to see and hear your movie.

iMovie automatically lowers the sound of the music in order to make the video clips audible. You can control the volume to get the right balance between the music and the video clip's audio.

5   In the timeline, tap the first video clip.

6   On the iPhone, tap the Inspector button 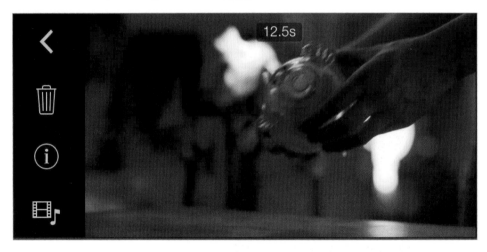.

The inspector is revealed below the timeline.

7   Tap Audio in the lower-left corner to show the Audio inspector.

In the Audio inspector, a volume slider controls the level of volume, and a mute button turns off the audio for the video clip.

8   Drag the volume slider left to lower the volume.

9   Tap the Play button to hear the new mix of audio. Tap the Pause button to stop playback.

10   Tap the green background music track in the timeline to open the Audio inspector for the track.

You can adjust the volume for the music track in the same manner you did for the video clip. You can also fade the music up or down.

11   To fade the music up or down, do the following:

▶   On the iPad, tap Fade in the lower right of the Audio inspector.

iPad

▶   On the iPhone, tap the Options button 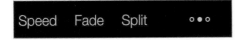, and then tap Fade.

Speed   Fade   Split   ○ ● ○

iPhone

The start and end of the music track now include yellow fade handles.

12 From the start of the music track, drag the yellow fade handle to the right to create a fade-in for the music.

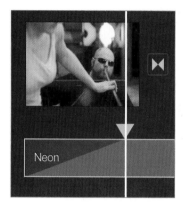

The shaded area at the start of the clip represents where the volume fades in.

13 Swipe to the start of the movie and tap the Play button to hear the music fade in.

To fade the music out, swipe to the end of the background music track and perform the same steps. For the end, drag the fade handle to the left.

You can add additional music or sound effects to your movie using audio provided by iMovie or your own audio content. Before you add it, you must remember to place the playhead.

14 Drag the timeline filmstrip so the playhead is located where you want audio to be added.

15 To access audio content, do the following:

▶ On the iPad, tap Audio above the browser.

▶ On the iPhone, tap the Media Browser button, and then tap Audio below the browser.

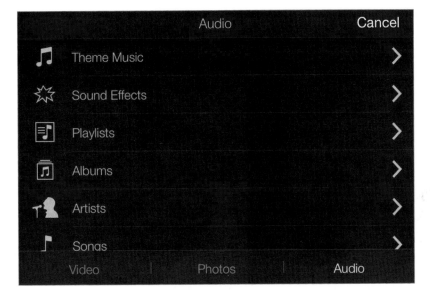

Audio is divided up among three sources:

▶ Tap Theme Music to select new theme music for your movie.

▶ Tap Sound Effects to add sound effects to your movie.

▶ Tap Playlists, Albums, Artists, or Songs to add music from your iTunes library.

NOTE ▶ iTunes songs marked Unavailable must be downloaded to your device for use in iMovie. After downloading, if a song on your device still appears unavailable, it may be protected by digital rights management and cannot be used in iMovie.

16 Tap Sound Effects to see a list of the sound effects.

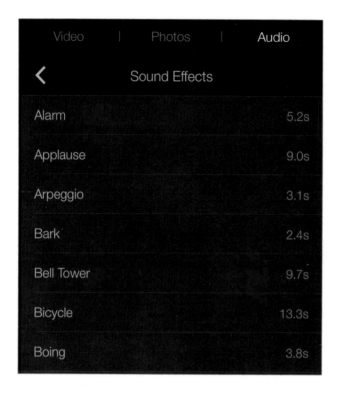

17   Swipe through the list and find a sound that may fit your movie—for instance, a crowd cheer if you're doing a sports movie.

18   Tap the sound effect to show the controls. Then tap the Play button to hear the sound.

Adding a sound effect is similar to adding a video clip.

19   Tap the arrow button in the sound effect controls to add the sound effect.

Sound effects (or any audio track except the background music track) are added to the timeline as a blue bar.

TIP ▶ To replace the existing background track with a blue audio track, select the blue audio track, and then tap the Options button in the Audio inspector. Then tap Move to Background, and your selected track replaces the existing background music track.

20 Drag the timeline filmstrip so the playhead is located before the start of the sound effect, and then tap the Play button to play your movie with the new sound.

TIP ▶ To quickly move to the start of the timeline, touch and hold on the far left edge of the timeline. To move to the end of the timeline, touch and hold on the far right edge of the timeline.

The new audio track can use the Audio inspector to adjust volume and fade the track in and out.

Applying Transitions and Titles

Up until now the theme has had very little impact on your movie except for the music. Themes play a much larger role when you start adding and changing transitions.

1 Skim to locate the first transition in the timeline.

Transitions appear as small boxes between each clip in the timeline.

2 Tap the transition to select it.

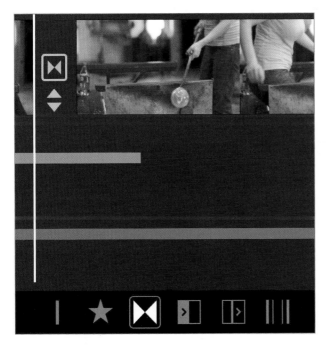

The transitions automatically added by iMovie as you add clips are cross dissolves. Cross dissolves are the most-used type of transition. They smooth out rough-looking changes or cuts between two clips in the timeline, but you may not want one between every cut in the timeline. You remove transitions by setting the transition type to None.

3   On the iPhone, tap the Inspector button to reveal the transition controls.

4   Tap the None button 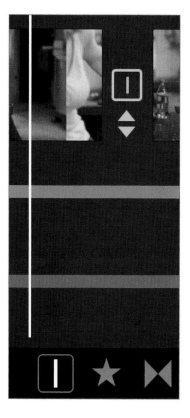 to remove the selected cross dissolve and change it to a cut between the two clips.

5   Play over the new cut to view the change.

6   Skim to another cross dissolve in the timeline and tap it to select it.

7   On the iPhone, tap the Inspector button to reveal the transition controls.

The cross dissolve is not the only transition type you can add. iMovie includes three other standard types and one designed to fit your theme.

8   Tap the Theme transition button ★ to change the current selected transition to the custom theme transition.

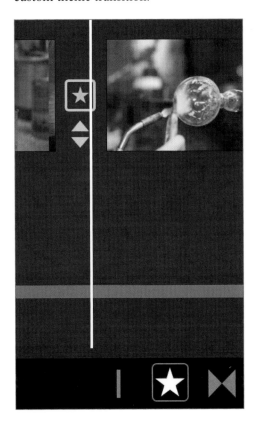

TIP   **TIP** ▶ Enable transition sound effects by tapping the Audio button in the Transition inspector.

9   Play the new theme transition to view it.

You can change how long the transition takes to complete from half-second, quick transitions to longer transitions up to 2 seconds.

10 Tap the theme transition to select it.

11 In the inspector tap the duration.

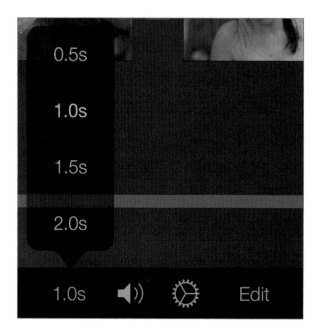

12 In the popover, tap the desired length, and then tap the duration in the inspector to hide the popover.

NOTE ▶ Occasionally, not all the transition lengths will be available in the menu. If the selection range on the clip you choose to add to your movie doesn't leave 2 seconds at the start of the clip and/or at the end of a clip, a 2-second transition cannot be created and that option won't show in the menu.

The other standard transitions can be applied and modified the same way. You can tap the Slide, Wipe, or Fade through (Black or White) to apply any of them to the selected transition. Using transitions requires a certain amount of restraint. Your movie is about your *video clips*, not iMovie transitions. Watching a movie that uses every transition type may be fun the first few times, but trust me—six months from now, it will lose its novelty. Stick to cross dissolves and one other transition type in your movies.

Fading a Movie In and Out

You can add transitions at the start and end of the movie to fade it in and fade it out. These transitions do not have different styles and are applied in a slightly different way.

1 Tap the Project Settings button below the timeline.

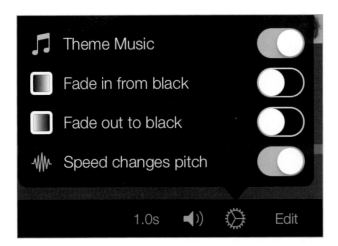

2   To fade the movie in when it starts, tap the "Fade in from black" switch.

3   To fade the movie out at the end, tap the "Fade out to black" switch.

4   Tap the Project Settings button again to hide the popover.

Using these switches to fade a movie in and out adds a nice bit of polish to it.

Applying Titles

Titles are another area where the theme you choose determines the look of your titling options.

1   In the timeline, tap the first clip.

2   On the iPhone, tap the Inspector button.

3   Tap Video to open the Video inspector.

4   On the right side of the inspector, tap Title to reveal the titling options.

5   For the first clip in the movie, tap Opening.

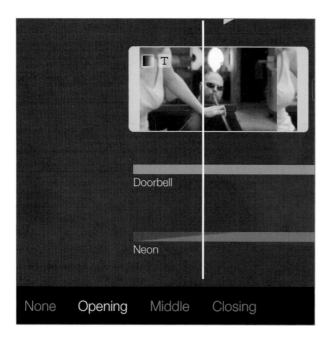

The opening title is meant to be the main title of your movie. The middle and closing title options are intended for placement in their respective movie locations (although they don't have to go there). For instance, you can place the middle title on the first clip if you want. The names are just guidelines based on the design of the titles. The theme's opening title design is applied by default when tapping the opening title option.

6   Tap the Title button $\boxed{\text{T}}$ to view additional title styles.

The selected title style is shown with a blue outline. Each title style thumbnail provides a style and movement preview.

7   Tap a title style to replace the existing opening theme title style.

8   Play the selected clip to view the newly applied style.

Once the title style is applied, you can enter your own text.

9   Tap on the text in the viewing area to select it.

TIP Once you select the text in the viewing area, you can tap twice to select a word, or three times to select all the text in the viewing area.

10   Delete the placeholder text and type your own title. When you've finished, tap Done.

As you add your titles and transitions, your theme can have a significant impact on the look of your movie. If you use alternative transitions and title styles, it can have no impact at all.

Switching Themes

Even if you chose to use the theme transition and title styles, your starting theme isn't the one you have to end with. If you apply a new theme to your movie, all the titles and transitions based on the original theme will switch to the new one.

1   Tap the Project Settings button.

2   In the Project Settings window, tap the new theme you want to apply.

TIP Choosing the Simple theme removes uses of standard cross dissolves, "Fade through black" transitions, and basic titles.

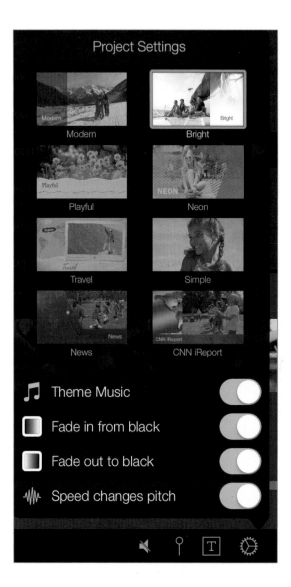

3   To close the Project Settings window do the following:

   ▶   On the iPad, tap the Project Settings button.

   ▶   On the iPhone, tap Done in the upper right of the screen.

4   Play the movie to view it with the newly applied theme.

Your movie has a new look, and it took just a few seconds to apply it. Don't be afraid to try different titles, transitions, or entire new themes on a movie. It's part of the fun!

Using Photos in a Movie

Most of us have more photos than we do video clips. Adding photos to your movies can be a great way to create a more advanced slideshow than you can in iPhoto.

1   To view your photos, do the following:

▶   On the iPad, tap Photos at the top of the media browser.

▶   On the iPhone, tap the Media Browser button, and then tap Photos at the bottom of the media browser.

The browser shows your Camera Roll and any albums from the Photos app, as well as any photos in iPhoto for iOS.

2   Tap any album, event, or the Camera Roll to access individual photos.

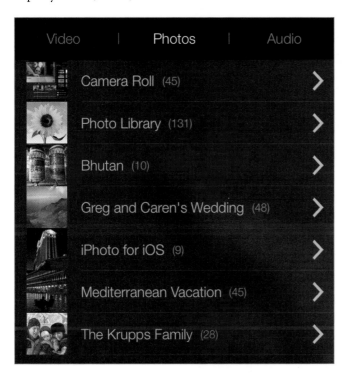

3   To add a photo at the current playhead position in the timeline, tap the photo in the media browser.

Unlike with video clips, you don't select a range of the photo to add. Photos by their very nature are just a single frame, so there's no range to select. Photos are added to the timeline with a default 6-second duration. If you want a shorter or longer duration, you can trim it in the timeline.

4   In the timeline, tap the photo to select it.

5   Drag the left or right edge selection handle to shorten or lengthen the photo's duration.

   TIP The photo's duration is displayed at the top of the viewing area, and it updates as you trim the photo using the selection handles.

Trimming is an important skill to master. It's a simple task with a still photograph, but you'll explore it more with video clips later in this lesson.

Modifying the Ken Burns Effect

Photos are added to the timeline with the Ken Burns effect—a slow pan-and-zoom motion. You can change the pan-and-zoom movement to better frame the subject in the photo.

> **NOTE** ▶ Why is it called the Ken Burns effect? Ken Burns is a filmmaker famous for his PBS documentaries. Many of his documentaries use archival photographs, and he popularized a technique that focuses attention and creates movement by panning and zooming the camera on the photographs.

1   In the timeline, tap the photo to select it.

The viewing area displays the controls for the Ken Burns effect.

2   In the viewing area, tap the Start button to position the playhead at the start of the photo in the timeline.

Use the controls to scale and position the photo as you want it to start when it plays in the timeline, and then switch to scale and position it as you want it to end in the timeline. iMovie will then figure out how to get from the starting position to the ending position.

3   Pinch the photo to shrink or scale it to the starting size you want in the viewing area.

4   Drag to position it within the frame.

TIP ▶ There is no automatic way to remove the Ken Burns effect altogether. The only way to remove it is to set the same size and position for both the start and end.

When you have the starting position set, you can switch to work on the end.

5   In the viewing area, tap the End button to position the playhead at the end of the photo in the timeline.

6   Pinch and drag the photo to scale and position it how you want in the viewing area.

7   In the viewing area, tap the Controls button to hide the Ken Burns controls.

Now your movie has a new look, and in the next exercise you'll experience it in all its full-screen glory.

Advanced Movie-Making Options

You've mastered most of the basic movie-making skills but now you're at a point where you can refine your movies into masterpieces. Many of the features you'll uncover in this section are not necessary for every movie; however, using them can elevate your movies into sparkling finished productions and make them more enjoyable to watch.

Learning to Trim

Trimming is similar to selecting the initial range when you add a clip to the timeline. Only now you are refining that selection in the timeline.

1   In the timeline tap a clip you want to trim.

When trimming you can add or remove frames from the start or end of each clip.

2   Drag the yellow handle at the start of the clip.

When you drag this handle to the left, you're adding frames to the beginning of the clip in the timeline and making the clip longer. If you drag to the right, you're removing frames from the clip and making it shorter.

> **TIP** ▶ Use the same process to trim audio tracks.

3   Drag the yellow handle at the end of the clip.

When you drag this handle to the left, you're removing frames from the end of the clip in the timeline and making the clip shorter. If you drag to the right, you're adding frames to the clip and making it longer.

> **TIP** ▶ iMovie will stop trimming when you've reached the end of the recorded video clip.

The viewing area updates to show you the first or last frame of the clip, depending on whether you are dragging at the start or end of the clip.

Trimming with Precision (iPad Only)

Basic trimming, as just described, suffices for most home movies. If your movie has more action or has a lot of talking, you might need to use a more sophisticated editing technique.

1   In the timeline tap a transition to select it.

2   Tap the yellow double arrows below the selected transition to open the precision editor.

The precision editor provides a magnified view of the transition between the two clips. The yellow and blue bars in the center indicate where the cut occurs between the two clips. The top filmstrip (also called the outgoing clip) is the clip before the transition and the bottom filmstrip (also called the incoming clip) is the clip after the transition.

NOTE ▶ If there is a cross dissolve or other transition, the yellow bars show the start and end points for the transition. If there is a cut between the two clips, the bars appear at the same point in the timeline.

3   Tap the Play button to view the cut between the two clips. Tap the Pause button to stop.

The shaded parts of the filmstrips in the upper-right and lower-left areas of the clips show portions of the clips that aren't used in the timeline.

4   Drag the yellow bar on the upper filmstrip to the right.

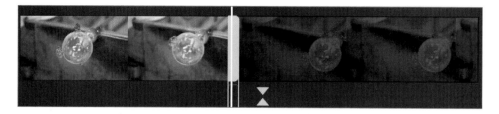

This is the same as trimming the end of the clip to the right as you did previously. You're adding to the end of the clip.

5   Drag the yellow bar on the lower filmstrip to the right.

This is the same as trimming the start of the clip to the right as you did previously. You're removing from the start of the clip.

6   When you've finished working in the precision editor, tap the double arrows to close it.

When you feel like you've mastered the two trims you just performed, you can do them simultaneously.

7   Tap to select a transition. Then tap the double arrows to enter the precision editor.

8   Drag the transition icon between the two filmstrips.

Dragging the transition icon left or right trims both clips at this transition. Instead of trimming each clip individually in the same direction, you're trimming them simultaneously.

Making a Split Edit

The precision editor can also trim the audio portion of each video clip. To make a more pleasing cut between two clips, it helps to have the audio of a video clip begin slightly before the video, or have audio of a clip continue slightly after the video ends. For example, a clip of an interviewer asking a question might cut early to the video of the person about to answer. The last few words of the question are heard but we see the person who is about to answer.

NOTE ► The precision editor is available only when using iMovie for iPad.

1   Still in the precision editor from the previous exercise, tap the Show Audio Wave-forms button ▄▟▖ to show the audio associated with the video clips.

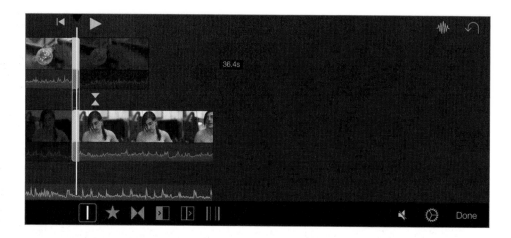

2   Drag the upper filmstrip's blue bar to the right.

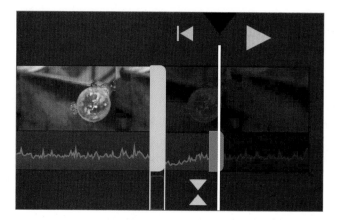

The blue bar indicates where the audio for the clip ends. Moving it to the right causes the video to end earlier than the audio for the outgoing clip.

3   Drag the lower filmstrip's blue bar to the right so it aligns under the top blue bar.

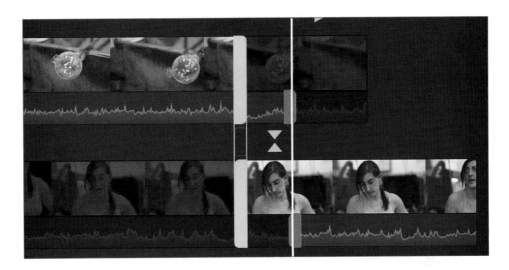

Moving the lower blue bar to the right causes the video to start earlier than the audio for the incoming clip. Since the blue bars are aligned when the outgoing clip's audio ends, the audio of the incoming clip starts when the outgoing audio ends.

4   Tap the double arrows to close the precision editor.

The precision editor is a powerful professional-style trimming tool that is essential for trimming interviews and dramatic movies.

Adding Cutaways

If part of a video clip is out of focus, or includes a few seconds not to your liking, but you want to keep the audio, you can cover up the unwanted video portion using a different video clip. This technique, called a cutaway, is often used in professional television and movie productions.

1   In the timeline, tap a clip that contains great audio but a few seconds of unwanted video.

2 Position the playhead where you want the cutaway clip to begin covering up the time-line video.

3 Return to the media browser and tap Video to view all your video clips.

When choosing a clip for a cutaway, you typically look for a clip that has some relevance to the audio on the selected clip in the timeline. For instance, if the clip in the timeline has someone speaking about a graduation, a good cutaway clip might be a clip of the graduation or the building where the graduation took place, or even a photo of the diploma.

4 In the browser tap a clip that will make a good cutaway.

5 Select the range of the clip in the browser, based on the length you want to cover up in the timeline.

6 On the iPad, tap the Options button ••• in the popover.

There are four alternative options for placing clips into the timeline:

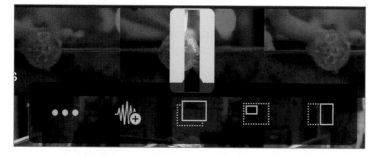

▶ Audio only ▦: Only audio from the browser clip is added to the timeline.

▶ Cutaway ▭: The browser clip is used to "cut away" from the main timeline clip.

▶ Picture-in-Picture ▫: The browser clip is inset over the main timeline clip.

▶ Split Screen ▯: The browser clip is shown on half the viewing area while the main timeline clip is shown on the other half.

7   Tap the Cutaway button.

The cutaway is added above the main clips in the timeline. The three video editing functions from the Options popover are called overlays because they overlay the main clips in the timeline.

Zooming In on a Clip

I'm sure there are times you wish you got closer to some action to record better video clips. Well, iMovie can put you closer to the action, at least in your movie.

1   In the timeline tap a clip you want to zoom in on.

A zoom control button is added to the lower-right corner of the viewing area.

2 Tap the zoom control to turn on the controls.

3 Pinch in the viewing area to zoom in on the picture.

4 Drag in the viewing area to position it.

TIP Tap twice in the viewing area to reset the clip back to its original size.

5   Tap the zoom control to turn off the controls.

Zooming in much beyond 20% of the original size will show some video degradation. The zoom controls don't replace a zoom lens or moving yourself closer to the action, but they can come in handy in a pinch.

Creating Slow Motion and Freeze Frames

When your movies have action you really want to show off, nothing beats showing it in slow motion. Whether you're showing sports action or leaps from a dance recital, add a few slow-motion clips and your viewers will be riveted.

1   In the timeline tap a clip you want to show in slow motion.

2   On the iPhone, tap the Inspector button.

3   In the Video inspector, tap Speed.

TIP ▶ iMovie can change the speed of a clip to be faster or slower, but not all iOS devices can perform all speeds.

4   Drag the speed slider to the left so the clip plays slower, or to the right so it plays faster.

5   Tap the Play button to see the speed change of the clip.

If you want to stop the action in "mid-air," you can create a freeze frame.

6   Position the playhead on the frame where you want to stop the action.

7   In the timeline tap the clip to select it.

8 In the Video inspector, tap Freeze.

iMovie inserts a 1-second freeze frame at the position of the playhead. If the playhead is in the middle of a clip, the freeze frame splits the clip, inserting itself in the middle.

Saving and Moving Projects

Anytime you make a project, iMovie automatically saves it into the project view. If you want to keep your projects only on the iOS device where you create them, your work is done. However, to get your movies out to your friends and family, you need to share them.

1 While viewing a movie or trailer, tap the Back button ◀ to view the project detail screen.

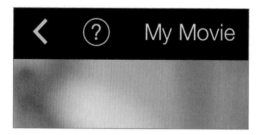

2 In the project detail screen, tap the movie or trailer title to enter a new one.

3   Tap the Share button .

You used the Share popover in Lesson 11 to share a clip to Facebook. In this lesson, you'll share your clip as a movie you can put on your Mac and as a project you can send to another iOS device.

4   Tap Save Video.

You can select an export size for your movie. If you recorded all your video on your iPhone, you'll want to choose the best possible quality for export.

5   In the popover, tap HD 1080P.

Once the movie is finished exporting, it is saved to your Camera Roll in the Photos app, where you can easily import to your Mac by connecting your iOS device and opening iPhoto.

If you want to move your project onto a different iOS device to continue editing, you can do that through iTunes.

6   Still in the project detail view, tap the Share button again.

7   Tap iTunes to begin sharing to iTunes.

Once the movie is finished sharing, you can use the file sharing features built into iTunes to transfer the project to another iOS device.

8   Connect your iOS device to your Mac or Windows PC, and then open iTunes.

9   In the upper-right corner of the iTunes window, select the iOS device.

10   Click the Apps button to show the apps installed on the device.

11   In the File Sharing section, select iMovie.

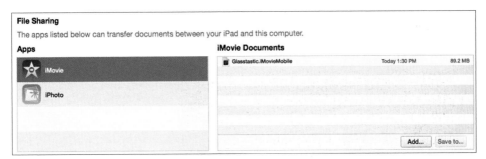

The iMovie Documents area shows files that have been shared to iTunes from iMovie for iOS.

12   Select the project you just shared, and then click the "Save to" button.

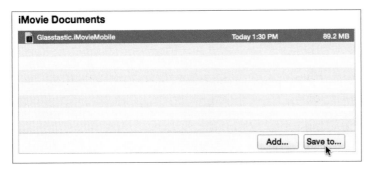

This save location is just a temporary holding place until you transfer the project file to another iOS device.

13 Save the file in a place where it will be easy to find later.

Sending a project to iTunes collects all the video clips, photos, and audio clips used in the project and copies them onto your Mac or PC temporarily. When your project and all of its associated media are transferred to a new iOS device, you can continue editing.

14 Once the project is saved, disconnect the device from your Mac or PC.

Now you'll connect the new device and transfer the project.

Connect your device to your computer, and then open iTunes on your computer.

15 Connect the new device to iTunes, and then select it from the top of the iTunes window.

16 Click the Apps button and select iMovie from the File Sharing section.

17 Click the Add button, and in the window that appears, select the project you saved earlier, and then click Open.

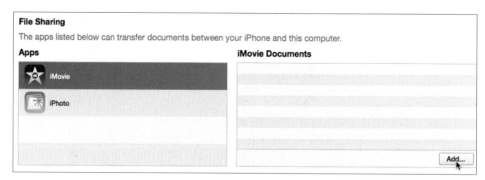

The project copies into the iMovie Documents pane in iTunes. Depending on the size of the project, this might take a few minutes.

18 In iMovie on your new iOS device, tap Projects at the top of the screen.

If you're editing a project, tap the Back button until you return to the Projects browser.

19 Tap the Import button , and then tap the name of the project from the popover.

Cancel   Edit

IMPORT PROJECTS FROM ITUNES

Glasstastic

When the import is finished, the project opens. You're ready to continue editing. The original project still exists on the device you created it on. In the next exercise, you'll learn how to delete it.

Deleting Clips and Projects

Deleting clips and projects can be a fairly disconcerting event. You're removing precious clips that will be gone forever, unless you've backed them up to your Mac or PC.

As you learned in Lesson 11, iMovie gets most of its clips through the Photos app after you record on the iPhone or iPad. These clips cannot be deleted in iMovie; they must be deleted in the Photos app. Only clips recorded using the iMovie camera discussed in Lesson 12 can be deleted in iMovie. These clips are considered "local media."

1   In iMovie, open a project that contains clips you recorded using the iMovie camera.

2   In the media browser, tap Video to view all the clips.

3   Tap the disclosure triangle and choose "Manage local media."

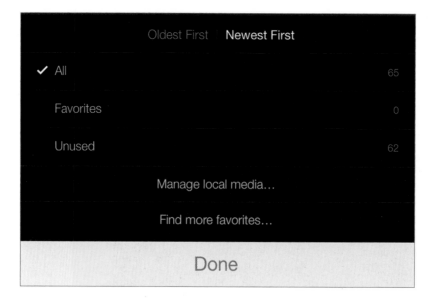

Most clips dim in the browser, except clips that have been recorded directly or imported into iMovie.

The local media clips are displayed with two buttons: Save and Delete.

4   To save a clip to the Camera Roll, tap Save.

Clips saved to the Camera Roll will no longer be available to delete in iMovie.

5   To remove a clip from iMovie and your iOS device, tap Delete.

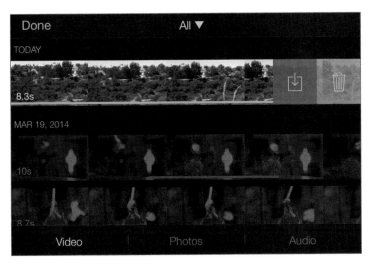

An alert appears, asking whether you want to delete the clip. You can either tap the alert to confirm the deletion of the clip, or tap anywhere else on the screen to cancel.

6   At the top of the browser, tap Done to return to viewing all the clips.

TIP ▶ Clips that have been used in a project will appear dim in the browser and will not be available to delete. You must remove "local media" clips from a project in order to delete them in iMovie.

Deleting projects is more straightforward.

7   In project detail view, tap the Trash button.

8   Tap Delete Project in the alert.

Video clips recorded into the project using the iMovie camera are also deleted from the iOS device unless you save them to the Camera Roll.

Access the Bonus Lesson: Sharing to iMovie Theater

This guide covered a lot of ground. I hope the moments you record are that much more enjoyable after learning a few things about iMovie and moviemaking. A lot of fun is to be had just sitting back and viewing your video clips in the browser, without ever having to make a movie. Turning those moments into short movies or trailers just adds to the fun you can have, while you're on the go on your mobile device. But nothing will bring you more joy than sharing those moments with the important people in your life. A Bonus lesson designed for this book can enhance the sharing experience by using iMovie Theater. iMovie Theater is a library of all the movies and trailers you've made and uses iCloud to automatically share them to all your devices, even your Apple TV.

For those using the eBook, you'll find all Bonus lesson after the index. For those using the printed book, you can access the Bonus lesson online.

To access the iMovie iOS Bonus lesson:

1   Connect to the Internet on your Mac or PC, navigate to www.peachpit.com/redeem, and enter your access code.

2   Click Redeem Code, and sign in or create a Peachpit.com account.

3   Locate the iMovie iOS Bonus lesson link on your Account Page under the Lesson & Update Files tab.

4   Click the iMovie iOS Bonus lesson link and download it to your Mac or PC Downloads folder.

5   After downloading the file, open your Downloads folder, and double-click the iMovie iOS Bonus.zip to unzip it.

    The Bonus lesson is provided in PDF form.

Lesson Review

1. True or false? Clips are always added to the end of the timeline.

2. Where are sound effects found in iMovie?

3. True or false? You remove a transition from the timeline by tapping the Trash icon.

4. How do you add theme music to a project?

5. How do you view clips in full screen?

6. How do you adjust the pan-and-zoom effect on a photo in the timeline?

7. Where can you slow down a clip in a project?

8. True or false? You move projects with all the project's clips from an iPhone to an iPad for further editing.

9. Why are some clips dimmed in the browser when you try to delete them?

10. What happens to clips recorded in iMovie when you delete the project they are in?

Answers

1. False. Clips are added to the timeline at the location of the playhead.

2. In the media browser, tap Audio and tap the Sound Effects category.

3. False. You remove a transition from the timeline by tapping the None transition type in the inspector.

4. Tap the Project Settings button, and then tap the switch for Theme Music.

5. In the playback controls, tap the Play Full Screen button.

6. In the timeline, tap the photo, and then tap the Start button. Pinch and drag the photo to a starting position. Tap the End button, and then pinch and drag the photo to an ending position.

7. In the Video inspector

8. True. Saving the project to iTunes and using iTunes file sharing allows you to transfer projects from one iOS device to another.

9. The clips are saved in the Photos app, not in iMovie.

10. The clips recorded in iMovie are deleted with the project.

34.1s

Index

OS X Support Essentials 10.9
Supporting and Troubleshooting OS X Mavericks

Kevin M. White, Gordon Davisson

Lesson and media files available for download

Logic Pro X
Professional Audio Production

David Nahmani

Lesson and media files available for download

al **Cut Pro X**
d Edition
nal Video Editing

ynand

The Apple Pro Training Series

Apple offers comprehensive certification programs for creative and IT professionals. The Apple Pro Training Series is both a self-paced learning tool and the official curriculum of the Apple Training and Certification program, used by Apple Authorized Training Centers around the world.

To see a complete range of Apple Pro Training Series books, videos and apps visit: **www.peachpit.com/appleprotraining**

Apple
Certified

Differentiate yourself. Get Apple certified.

Stand out from the crowd. Get recognized for your expertise by earning Apple Certified Pro status.

Why become an Apple Certified Pro?

Raise your earning potential. Studies show that certified professionals can earn more than their non-certified peers.

Distinguish yourself from others in your industry. Proven mastery of an application helps you stand out in a crowd.

Display your Apple Certification logo. With each certification you get a logo to display on business cards, resumés, and websites.

Publicize your certifications. Publish your certifications on the Apple Certified Professionals Registry (training. apple.com/certification/records) to connect with clients, schools, and employers.

Learning that matches your style.

Learn on your own with this Apple Pro Training Series book from Peachpit Press. Advanced titles and video training are also available for select topics.

Learn in a classroom at an Apple Authorized Training Center (AATC) from Apple Certified Trainers providing guidance.

Visit **training.apple.com** to find Apple training and certifications for:

OS X	Aperture
OS X Server	Pages
Final Cut Pro X	Numbers
Logic Pro X	Keynote

 Training and Certification